CROWOOD SPORTS GUIDES
TABLE TENNIS
SKILLS • TECHNIQUES • TACTICS

CROWOOD SPORTS GUIDES
TABLE TENNIS
SKILLS • TECHNIQUES • TACTICS

Jenny Heaton

THE CROWOOD PRESS

First published in 2009 by
The Crowood Press Ltd
Ramsbury, Marlborough
Wiltshire SN8 2HR

www.crowood.com

British Library Cataloguing-in-Publication Data
A catalogue record for this book is available from the British Library.

ISBN 978 1 84797 090 9

Dedication
To my husband John for his help with the proof reading and support throughout the project.

Acknowledgements
The author and publishers would like to thank the following for their help in the production of this book: Jill Parker MBE and Don Parker, the players at the National Centre for their time and expertise, and the ETTA and ITTF.

The photographs that appear in the book were taken by David Weam.
Line drawings by Keith Field.

Disclaimer
Please note that the author and the publisher of this book are not responsible or liable, in any manner whatsoever, for any damage, or injury of any kind, that may result from practising, or applying, the techniques and methods and/or following the instructions described in this publication. Since the exercises and other physical activities described in this book may be too strenuous in nature for some readers to engage in safely, it is essential that a doctor is consulted before undertaking such exercises and activities.

Typeset by Bookcraft, Stroud, Gloucestershire
Printed and bound in Malaysia by Times Offset (M) Sdn Bhd

CONTENTS

PREFACE

Table tennis is a fun and exciting game enjoyed by people of all ages and from all walks of life. Anyone can enjoy playing table tennis, but to be good at table tennis like any other sport requires dedication, coaching and training. It is a very accessible sport and it is widely played throughout the world. The International Table Tennis Federation started with only five countries in 1926, England being one of these. Now there are over 200 member-country associations.

Table tennis has been an Olympic sport for both singles and doubles events since the Seoul games in 1988; in 2008 in Beijing, team events were included for both men's and women's national teams.

Table tennis can be played in most leisure centres and there are leagues in nearly every major town. There are over 150 premier clubs registered in England. Some clubs are still based in church halls or business facilities, but all of the premier clubs are table tennis specific clubs, which have their own premises or are based in leisure centres. Even the Members of Parliament have their own team at the House of Commons.

Table tennis is classed as a 'high fidelity sport', which means that once a person has become involved they are likely to remain involved for longer than in many other sports. In other words, once you are hooked you'll stay hooked!

Table tennis is often a lifelong sport; in the World Veteran Championships there are people competing in over-40, 50, 60, 70, 75, 80 and over-85 age categories.

At the top level, table tennis is one of the fastest games to play and involves an enormous amount and variety of spin. At this level more than two strokes can be played in one second, at speeds over 100mph (160kph) and the ball can rotate up to 100 times per second. It is also a very tactical game, involving trying to out-manoeuvre and deceive an opponent in order to win a point. It has often been referred to as being like 'playing chess at 100 miles an hour'. So to play table tennis at this level you need to be smart as well as sharp!

Whether you just want to have some fun hitting the ball once in a while, or you want to be really good, then as in any sport you need to train in a systematic way. This book aims to provide the necessary information to help both beginners and existing players to do just that. A good technique will result in a better player and make it more rewarding and challenging. This guide provides all the technical and tactical information needed to enable a beginner or an experienced player to improve their game and reach their full potential. The physical requirements of the game are also included as these are an integral part of playing any sport to the full.

This guide will also appeal to coaches, as it provides a good resource of technical, tactical and on- and off-the-table training information that will be useful to them in their coaching work.

Diagram Key

On all table diagrams in this guide:

Arrows = direction and path of the ball
BH = Backhand stroke
FH = Forehand stroke

PART I

INTRODUCTION TO TABLE TENNIS

CHAPTER 1

A BRIEF HISTORY AND THE BASIC RULES

Table tennis is believed to have been devised in the 1880s as an adaptation of lawn tennis that could be played on the dining room table. The first patents were registered in the 1880s and were sold with simple rules. Ping Pong was named after the sound the ball made, and Whiff-Waff after the sound of the moving racket, so it is believed.

Rubber and cork balls were used in these early versions, but in 1900 these were replaced with celluloid ones. The first books on the game were published in 1901 and the English Table Tennis Association (ETTA) was officially formed in 1927, the same year that the first World Championships were held, in London.

England had many world champions in the early days of the sport, often referred to as the 'hard bat' era because the bat coverings did not include a sponge layer. The most notable English players of this era were Fred Perry, the world singles champion in 1929 who later went on to play lawn tennis, winning eight Grand Slam tennis titles including three at Wimbledon, and Johnny Leach, who won the world table tennis singles twice (in 1949 and 1951).

At the beginning of the 1950s, a new force from Asia began to take over from the Europeans and this was led by the 'whirlwinds' from Japan with their high-speed style. Despite this influence, England continued to be a force in table tennis, winning the men's World Team Championships (the Swaythling Cup) in 1953 and the women's world doubles title in 1951 and 1954 by the 'Rowe Twins' (Ros and Di).

Di Rowe also won the European team title in 1958 with Ann Haydon who, like Fred Perry, went on to play tennis and win the singles title at Wimbledon. Di Rowe also went on to win the European doubles

title twice more with Mary Shannon in 1962 and 1964.

During the 1960s and 1970s the 'modern era' of table tennis emerged, with the development of the large array of high-tech bats used today.

Among some of the most successful English players in the modern era were Desmond Douglas, who was one of the most feared competitors of the late 1970s and 1980s; John Hilton, winner of the European Championships in 1980; and Jill Parker, who in 1976 won the European singles title and teamed up with Linda Howard to take the women's doubles crown.

This brief look at the history of English table tennis wouldn't be complete without mentioning Chester Barnes, who became one of the most recognizable sportsmen of the 1960s. He played with an unusual square-shaped bat and won the national men's title at the age of fifteen. He was a flamboyant character, always entertaining to watch, but he never achieved the wins outside England that his talent promised. He was the first table tennis player to surround himself with an 'entourage' which included his own manager and photographer, and a number of loyal fans. After retiring from table tennis he went on to forge an extremely successful career as a racehorse trainer at the stables of the 15-times champion trainer Martin Pipe.

It wasn't long before the Chinese began to dominate the world game, a position which they still hold today. This is hardly surprising since they have over 20 million players to choose from! The first of the many world champions to come from China that the author remembers seeing was Chang Tse Tung, who played in front of a packed crowd at the Central Hall, Birmingham, about forty years ago. Since then the Chinese have continued to dominate

the world scene and have had too many world champions to mention here. The Chinese women, in particular, have won most of the world titles for which they have competed.

In the 1980s and 1990s the European men made an impact on Chinese domination with players like Jan-Ove Waldner of Sweden regarded by many as the greatest player of all time; Jorgen Persson also of Sweden; Vladamir Samsonov from the Ukraine; Jean-Paul Gatien from France and most recently Timo Boll from Germany who were all ranked world number one at some time during this period.

The England men's team won the silver medal at the European Championships in Paris in 1988 only narrowly losing 5–3 to the Swedish men's team, who with the same team went on to win the World Championships in 1989 beating China 5–0 and retaining the title in 1991 and 1993.

Currently, England have a number of very promising young players such as Paul Drinkhall, Darius Knight and Gavin Evans who are making their mark in the game. In 2005 they won the Cadet (under-15) World Team Challenge and team gold at the European Youth Championships also at cadet level, and then at junior level in 2007.

A brief history such as this cannot mention all the great players from around the world but more information can be found on the ETTA and ITTF websites, the details of which are in Part 5.

The Basic Rules

The complete rules of the game are published by the International Table Tennis Federation (ITTF) and every player should familiarize themselves with them. They are available from the English Table Tennis

Association (ETTA) if you live in England, or from your home country association. Like all rule books they are very detailed so this chapter aims to provide a simplified summary of the rules for those new to the game.

Table tennis can be played between two players (singles) or four players (doubles). The players stand behind opposite ends of the table and the aim is to hit the ball over the net which is 6 inches (15cm) high so that it bounces on the opponent's side of the table.

A point begins with one player serving the ball by releasing it from the hand and hitting it with the racket. The ball must bounce on the server's side before going over the net and bouncing on the opponent's side. If the ball hits the net and still goes over (a let serve) the ball is served again. There is no restriction as to the number of let serves, unlike in lawn tennis.

The opponent then has to return the ball over the net before it bounces again. During a rally, the ball can only bounce once on each side of the net. The ball cannot be volleyed, again unlike in lawn tennis. If the ball misses the table on an opponent's side or doesn't clear the net then a point is lost.

The dimensions of a table tennis table are shown in Figure 1. The edge of the table top is deemed to be in play but not the sides. The ball can also be played around the net rather than over it and often is when a player is returning the ball away from the table.

There are additional rules for doubles play which relate mainly to the service. However, the most important thing to note about doubles play is that the players in the pair take turns to hit the ball and a point is lost if the ball is hit out of turn.

When serving in doubles, the ball must be struck from the right-hand half of the court and land in the opponent's right-hand court, that is, diagonally. If the service bounces anywhere else, on either side of the table, a fault is called and the server loses the point. Figure 1 shows how the centre line on a table divides each side into two halves.

Figure 2 (see page 10) shows the service changes in a doubles match. At each change of service, the previous receiver becomes the server and the partner of the previous server becomes the receiver.

KEY POINT

Summary of Basic Rules

A good service starts with the ball resting on the palm of the service hand (not the one holding the bat). The ball is thrown upwards at least 16cm (7in), and on its way down the server strikes the ball so that it touches first his side of the table (court) and then his opponent's side of the table (court).

A good return is where the ball, having been served, is struck so that it passes over the net (or around it) and bounces on the opposite side of the table (court).

A let occurs when the ball in service, in passing over the net, touches it and is otherwise good (it goes over the net and hits the receiver's side). The service is taken again.

Serving passes to the receiving player after two points have been played, except at 10 points all, when service is alternate.

A point is won if an opponent:

- Fails to make a good service or return
- Hits the ball before it has bounced when it is above or moving towards the playing surface
- Lets the ball bounce twice before hitting it
- Moves or touches the net with the free hand
- Hits the ball twice.

A game is won by the player first scoring 11 points (unless both players score 10 points, when the game is won by the first player subsequently gaining a lead of 2 points).

Order of service alternates with games, so that the player (or pair) serving first in a game will receive first in the next game of the match.

A match consists of the best of any odd number of games, such as best of 3, 5 or 7.

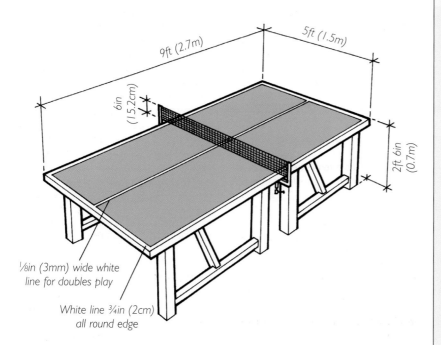

9ft (2.7m)

5ft (1.5m)

6in (15.2cm)

2ft 6in (0.7m)

⅛in (3mm) wide white line for doubles play

White line ¾in (2cm) all round edge

Figure 1 Markings and dimensions of a table tennis table.

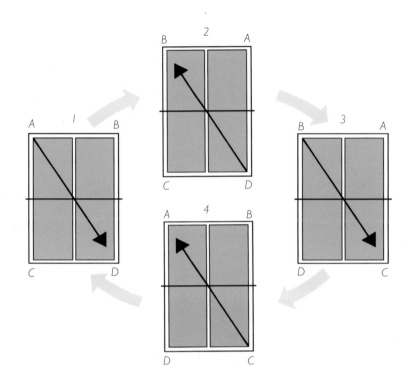

Figure 2 Service changes in doubles.

The umpire of a game may be another player or an officially qualified umpire who has undergone training and assessment in the laws of the game.

At the start of a game, the main responsibilities of the umpire are to ensure that a legal bat (with an ITTF stamp on the rubber) is being used and the net height is correct. During the game the umpire must ensure that the service technique is legal, all the rules are adhered to and that the service changes correctly. The umpire has to call the score out clearly or use scoreboards when available. The umpire may manually turn the score over on the board or sometimes electronic ones are used. The server's score is always called out first.

The free arm acts as a counter-balance to the movement forward towards the short ball.

CHAPTER 2

CLOTHING AND EQUIPMENT

Clothing

If you are new to the game of table tennis and playing within a leisure centre or at school then any sports clothing will suffice. However, it is important that the clothing is loose-fitting to allow freedom of movement as you engage in playing, just as for any other kind of physical activity.

As the game is played indoors it is most likely that you will sweat so it is advisable that the clothing is made of a material that absorbs perspiration and is easily washed and dried.

At competition level clothing normally consists of a short-sleeved or sleeveless shirt, shorts or skirt or one-part sports outfit (although these are rare in table tennis), socks and playing shoes. A tracksuit is not normally worn during play but may be allowed by agreement at local level or with the permission of the referee at tournament level. The main colour of the clothing, other than the sleeves and collar of a shirt, has to be clearly different from that of the ball. In the past this would only have been white as the balls were white but now balls of other colours, such as orange, are used. There are further rules about manufacturing logos and sponsorship markings which are set out in the ITTF rules.

A tracksuit for use when travelling to and from the venue or during a warm-up is also a useful part of your equipment. They are also useful for wearing during intervals between play as they will help to keep the body and particularly the limbs and muscles warm. This will help prevent injury. A tracksuit is also suitable for wearing during the pre-match knock-up but must be of a design that makes it easy to remove before the start of the match.

Footwear

Suitable footwear should always be worn and any footwear needs to have a well-defined tread to prevent slipping and avoid injury. The sole should also be non-marking, an essential requirement for use in many facilities. Lightweight footwear that offers good support, particularly around the heel and instep, is essential. Flexibility is also desirable as table tennis requires fast footwork with a lot of turning and changing of direction. Trainers are often quite rigid and for this reason they are not recommended. It is also important to replace your footwear as soon as it is past its best. Worn treads may result in slipping and injury and weakened support can cause a number of foot injuries.

There are a number of specialist stockists of table tennis equipment who sell specially developed footwear.

The choice of socks is also important. Sports socks are often thicker than normal socks so bear this in mind when you try on any footwear; better still, make sure you wear your chosen socks when buying your footwear. Seamless socks are usually more comfortable and will reduce rubbing.

Equipment

Blades

The 'blade' is the bat without the rubber. It can be of any size, shape or weight provided that the surface is flat and rigid; 85 per cent of the blade must be natural wood. Thin layers of carbon fibre are one substance that has been successfully used in blades, adding to the speed, but also to the cost.

In general, blades can be categorized as follows:

- Defensive Blade (slow)
- All-round Blade (medium and recommended for beginners)
- Offensive Blade (fast)
- Carbon Blade (very fast)
- Soft Wood or Harder Wood.

Faster blades tend to lose the 'feeling' required for touch shots such as a short push and they also make general control more difficult. Most top players tend to choose an all-round or an offensive blade, with faster rubbers to give them the extra speed whilst maintaining the feel and control required.

When starting to play, an all-round blade is the best one to buy, and then as you develop your game and style you will be in a better position to choose the right blade to suit your style of play.

TOP TIP

A towel to dry your forehead and hands is a must so that sweat doesn't go in your eyes or hamper your grip as this will affect your strokes and your ability to play well.

USEFUL TIP

Some floors can be slippery and many experienced players keep an old piece of cloth or towel in their bag which they dampen to reduce the risk of injury by stepping on to it between rallies.

		Faster		
Defensive blade (3 ply)	All-round blade (5 ply)	Offensive blade (7 ply)		Carbon blade

Figure 3 Speed comparison of blades.

Rubbers

The blade is usually covered with rubber which must have a matt finish and be black one side and red the other. Rubbers come in an incredible number of types and at a great variety of prices. Equipment with the ITTF logo from an established company will generally be of higher quality and is a requirement for participation in any official play, both nationally and internationally.

All rubbers have a smooth side and a pimpled side and most, although not all, are designed to be used in conjunction with a layer of sponge which is bonded to the rubber during manufacture.

The same type of rubber may be supplied with different thicknesses of sponge, normally ranging from 1.0mm to 2.5mm ($\frac{1}{24}$in to $\frac{3}{16}$in).

Other factors such as softness or hardness of the rubber–sponge combination and frictional properties determine the spin, speed and control characteristics.

There is a vast array of rubbers available but they generally fall into four categories:

- Reverse
- Short Pimples
- Long Pimples
- Anti-Spin.

Reverse Pimpled Rubber

By far the most used rubbers are reverse rubbers. With reverse rubbers, the playing surface is not pimpled because the pimples face inwards and are attached to a layer of sponge. Various combinations of sponge and the playing surface are available which will affect the spin, speed and control that the rubber produces. Generally, soft sponge rubbers are slower than hard sponge rubbers, though the introduction of 'speed glue' (see Gluing Your Rubber to the Blade, below) can alter that.

Short Pimples

Short pimples face outward and the sponge is attached to the smooth side. The pimples are short, as the name implies, and they are usually wider than long pimples and positioned closer together. They have relatively low frictional properties because less surface area comes in contact with the ball and are therefore limited in terms of producing spin.

For this reason short pimples are often only used on one side of the bat, usually the backhand, in order to produce the desired speed and control and also to counter the spin produced by an opponent.

Long Pimples

Long pimples face outward and are usually longer, thinner and further apart than short pimples. Long pimples will react in a very different way from all other rubbers and are somewhat unpredictable because of pimple recovery after the ball is struck. This will be explained in more detail later. They are also difficult to play against and

difficult to play with and alter significantly the technique required. For this reason this type of rubber is not recommended for beginners or until good technique is established.

Anti-spin

This is a reversed rubber and the smooth side is used for striking the ball. This rubber is characterized by having extremely low frictional properties combined with hard rubber. This results in very slow speed and virtually no spin but provides good control and the ability to counter spin effectively. However, these characteristics also hamper the range of effective stroke production and for this reason it is not recommended for beginners.

USEFUL TIP

Rubber needs to be changed much more regularly than blades, and will depend on the amount you play and the level you wish to play at.

Rubber should be maintained by cleaning with water at the end of the practice or match and have a cover to keep it dust-free and out of direct sunlight and high temperatures.

Gluing Your Rubber to the Blade

When starting to play you may buy a bat with the rubber already attached to the blade, but as you improve you will probably buy your blade and rubber separately, like most players, and therefore need to glue the rubber to the blade. Most table tennis suppliers will do this for you if you prefer but if you start to use 'speed glue' then it will be necessary to learn to glue your own.

For some time 'speed glue' has been used to increase the speed of the rubber and hence the speed of the ball. The use of 'soft sponge' underneath the rubber also increases the effect of the speed glue. The use of 'speed glue' reduces the amount of impact force between bat and

---

KEY POINT

To achieve the best early progress an all-round blade with reverse rubber having a sponge thickness of around 1.5mm ($\frac{1}{16}$in) is recommended as this will allow the basic strokes to be properly played.

Many sports shops and specialist table tennis suppliers also sell made up bats with the rubber already glued on. These are often cheaper and can be very good to start playing with, but make sure the rubber is reversed (playing side is smooth) and has a good grip so that you can impart spin on the ball otherwise you will be making it harder to develop your strokes and your game.

ball required to achieve the same speed and/or power and so reduces the length of the stroke, which of course in turn reduces the recovery time needed between strokes.

It may sound a long process but with practice it takes only minutes and many top players repeat the gluing process prior to every match they play to ensure the maximum effect of the 'speed glue'.

As from 2008 the use of glues containing volatile compounds (VCs) was banned and tested for at ITTF events. This ban was for health and safety reasons. All affiliated associations followed suit and testing soon began in all official events.

For the up-to-date position on the use of speed glues, visit the ITTF website.

The use of 'speed glue' too early in a player's development hinders good stroke production and long-term goals as it reduces the need to use the whole body

in the production of the attacking strokes. Whole-body action remains very important for ultimate speed and power, even when using 'speed glue'.

Balls

The ball is spherical and has a diameter of 40mm (1½in) and weighs 2.7g (¹⁄₁₀oz). The ball's diameter was increased in the 1990s in order to slow the game down and make it more appealing to spectators. The ball has to be celluloid or a similar plastic material and it is usually white or orange and must have a matt finish.

The quality of a table tennis ball is indicated by a star rating found on the balls, which may be 1*, 2* or 3*. The higher the star rating the higher the quality of the ball and the better the bounce will be. A good, consistent bounce makes it easier to learn and improve your play. The better quality balls also last longer provided you don't tread on them.

Tables

There are three types of table generally available: free-standing, rollaway with playback and rollaway.

A free-standing table has separate halves, each half supported on four legs. To avoid damage, the two halves need to be stored surface to surface. They are easier to transport and store than rollaway tables, but are more difficult and time-consuming to set up and take down.

A rollaway with playback table has a playing surface which is split into two halves, each one mounted on a central wheeled undercarriage to form one unit. In storage both halves are locked in a vertical position. Playback allows the player to practise alone by having one half down and the other vertical which is used to return the ball back to the player. Playback tables are easy to set

up, take down and manoeuvre but they are bulky to store.

A rollaway table is similar to the 'rollaway with playback' but the undercarriage is designed for easier storage. Some versions even have a separate undercarriage for each table half.

The thickness of the table top is important as it has an effect on the bounce of the ball. The thicker the top surface, the better the bounce will be. They vary from about 17mm to 24mm (¹¹⁄₁₆ to ¹⁵⁄₁₆in) with the recommended match-play thickness of 22mm (¹⁴⁄₁₆ in), but 19mm (¹²⁄₁₆in) will still provide a good bounce.

Traditionally the table surfaces were always coloured green with white lines but now they are often blue; very occasionally red ones have been used.

Nets and Surrounds

There are three types of removable net assembly, spring clamp and screw clamp, and fixed ones which form an integral part of the table. The spring and screw clamp types need to be removed prior to taking down the table. The fixed ones often get damaged in storage and stick out which can create a safety hazard.

Surrounds (barriers) are moveable and used to partition playing areas for match-play, practice or coaching sessions within a club situation or at tournaments. Figure 4 shows their use at a major tournament. For practising, coaching or club matches the area enclosed would be much smaller than shown in the photograph overleaf.

Figure 4 The use of table tennis barriers in a large hall.

CHAPTER 3

PLAYING THE GAME

Venues

Many of the new leisure centres in the UK are run by local authorities and some serve as a venue for school sports, opening to the public in the evenings and at weekends. Within these centres there are usually multi-purpose areas catering for several sports. Table tennis is often available and a table may be set up on a badminton court with a long curtain separating the remaining area in which another sport can be played. The advantage of table tennis is that a minimum of four tables can be set up on one badminton court and these can be separated using special table tennis barriers.

Often a table tennis club operates in one of these venues but some clubs now have specific premises for the sole use of a table tennis club. A club provides the opportunity of receiving coaching, meeting and playing with other players and competing as a member of a team. As a member of a club you can also take part in a number of other types of competition.

Another advantage of joining a club is cost, because over a season it can provide cheaper table tennis enjoyment and a lot more interest than going down to your local sports centre for 'pay and play'.

Many schools possess table tennis equipment and have their own teams that compete in both local leagues and school competitions. These are organized by the English Schools Table Tennis Association (ESTTA). Local leagues are sanctioned by the English Table Tennis Association (ETTA), and players pay an affiliation fee to both the county the club is in, mainly to help finance the county teams, and the ETTA. Many clubs generate income by setting an annual membership fee, determined by factors such as hall cost, cost of balls, frequency of club nights, number of members, and so on. The fee may or may not include team registration fees to the local league, but these are usually only paid by those members who wish to compete. Belonging to a club does not oblige a member to compete; many players just enjoy playing against their fellow members on club night.

If you decide to join a club, then it is very simple to find out the nearest ones to you by visiting the ETTA website. It is always worthwhile to visit each club before making your choice.

USEFUL TIP

Guidelines for Choosing a Club

- Decide how much time you have available to play and find out which club operates at the times you are free.
- Ask if there are club nights and how many tables are available for how many players.
- If you want to compete, find out how many teams the club runs and if there are likely to be vacancies in the teams.
- Ask what other facilities are available, such as separate changing rooms for men and women, and whether they have showers.
- Ask whether the club is affiliated and has insurance, or better still has achieved a 'Clubmark'.
- Ask if coaching is available.

Most table tennis clubs cater for players of all abilities and ages, and there are a number of clubs that have been designated as particularly suitable for disabled players. All the relevant information about affiliated clubs in England can be obtained from the ETTA website.

Club Etiquette

Each club will have its own system of play on club nights and this will be explained to you. Make sure that you know the etiquette by asking if you are unsure; if at the end of the session equipment needs to be put away, take your turn in helping.

There are usually designated match nights and in many clubs tables are not available for social use on these nights. However, some of the bigger clubs may have tables allocated for use on match nights so ask the question. It is important that you do not disturb players taking part in the matches.

The Competition Structure

Club members take part in local leagues which usually have their own league championships at the end of each season. There are also team cup competitions and inter-league opportunities in most areas.

Many players at some time will want to enter a tournament and the opportunity in table tennis is vast.

Tournaments

These are primarily individual events but often include men's and women's doubles competitions. Mixed doubles is not included in many tournaments now, but is still played at the National Championships, some international events, Commonwealth and World Championships. This omission is mainly due to the large entry in tournaments making it difficult to timetable a mixed doubles event. It is a pity as mixed doubles was a very popular event in the past and required very different tactics to men's and women's doubles.

If they are 'open' tournaments then anyone can enter. If they are 'restricted' tournaments then only players matching the set criteria will be allowed to enter. For instance, there are a number of tournaments that have age restrictions. At junior level there are tournaments for U18, U15 (known as cadets), U14, U13, U12 and U11. At senior level there are sometimes U21 categories. At veteran level there are over-40, 50, 60 and 70 categories and sometimes others are included. The World Veterans Championship has categories up to the over-85s.

Many open tournaments now have graded categories in addition to the open events, which are usually dictated by a player's national rating. These are very popular as they allow players to compete against others of the same standard.

The open tournaments are also graded for rating purposes; the higher the grade the higher the tournament rating, which means a player can gain more rating points.

1*, 2* and 3* tournaments are often regionally organized, but do not restrict players from other regions from entering if they wish. There are fewer 4* tournaments because the requirements to obtain this rating are more demanding, and these tend to be spread around the country.

There are Senior National Championships held annually which are restricted to those players who are eligible to play for England at veteran, senior and U21 level. There are also separately organized National Championships at junior and cadet level, and another one for the U11, U12, U13 and U14 age groups.

The other UK countries stage their own National Championships as do most ITTF affiliated countries.

Team Competitions

Other than local leagues, there are a number of other team competitions organized for clubs such as the British League, National League and National Club Championships. All these are competed for at senior, junior and cadet level for both females and males.

Players may also be selected to represent their county in the National County Championships or their league in the National Team Championships.

International Competitions

Most European countries have their own National League and many players from other countries take part and are paid to play for the participating clubs. One of the strongest of these is the Bundesliga in Germany.

There are a number of international open tournaments organized in many European countries as part of the foreign Pro Tour, and further afield as part of the World Pro tour.

There is a European League for national teams and a separate European Club Cup of Champions. There are also European Top 10 events for juniors and cadets and Top12 ones for seniors.

English players representing their country are also able to compete in the European and World Championships for team and individual honours at senior, junior and cadet level. England also competes in the Commonwealth Championships and as part of the British team in the Olympics. Prior to the Beijing Olympics 2008, there were four events in table tennis, two doubles and two singles, but since then team events have also been included for both males and females making six events in total.

English Schools Table Tennis Association (ESTTA)

This association is affiliated to the ETTA and supports team competitions at U11, U13, U16, and U19 levels for boys and girls. All schools, primary and secondary, whether in the public or private sector, are eligible to play.

The competition is organized firstly at county, then zone and regional levels culminating in the National School Team Championships. ESTTA also organizes the National Individual School Championships.

It is estimated that some 10,000 players take part at some stage in these competitions.

ESSTA representative players also take part in the Home Countries International events with the competing countries taking turns as host. ESSTA also has a key role in the promotion of World Schools Table Tennis competitions which are held bi-annually in different countries. Competitions have so far been held in Israel, Belgium, France, Slovakia, Germany and China.

The player focuses on the ball throughout the stroke.

A young player competing in one of the many 'open' tournaments.

CHAPTER 4

COACHING AND SKILLS AWARDS

Coaching

After starting to play table tennis you will probably receive some guidance from a teacher in school or a coach at an organized session in a leisure centre or club. If so, you will be aware of the benefits to be gained from being coached. However, what is surprising is that some of the better club players and particularly adults don't always recognize the benefits of being coached.

There is every advantage to be gained. No matter what standard a player is they will benefit from being observed, analysed and corrected by someone who can stand back, watch and help. The more experienced and qualified that person is the better the help will be. Like all professions there are the good and not so good, so by all means be selective and find out what experience and qualification a coach has.

Many clubs and certainly all Premier Clubs in England will have well-qualified and experienced coaches. There are also more advanced and 'personal performance' sessions organized both regionally and nationally. These are often by invitation only but there are a number of residential and non-residential courses organized by table tennis specialists open to any level or age of player.

Who are the Coaches?

Many players take up coaching because they want to put something back into the game that has given them so much enjoyment, whilst others view it as a career move and become full-time coaches working in schools, the community, clubs or at regional and national level. Whatever your level of play is you can help others with the right training. As a coach it is important to recognize your own limitations and

restrict your coaching to ability groups that suit your standard as a coach and player, and then both you and your pupils will benefit. This is because the more experienced you are as a player the more comfortable and able you'll feel imparting knowledge to others. That's not to say all good players make the best coaches, but it does help to have been a good player when coaching other good players.

Up until 2006, England had its own coaching qualifications as did all the other home countries, but now the United Kingdom Coaching Certificate has taken over. The UK Coaching Certificate is an endorsement of sport-specific coach education qualifications against agreed criteria across four levels, and has been adopted by most sports in the UK. The awarding body for these qualifications in England, Wales and Ulster is 1st4Sport and in Scotland it is the responsibility of Scottish Qualifications Authority (SQA).

Figure 6 outlines the coaching pathway for the UK, showing that each home country also has zero-level awards below the UKCC qualifications designed for players who want to act as club leaders or for teachers who want to start up table tennis in their school.

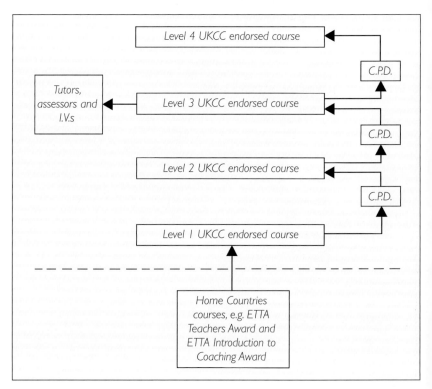

Figure 6 UK Coaching Pathway. C.P.D. = continued professional development; I.V. = internal verifier.

TABLE 1: UKCC ENDORSED COACHING QUALIFICATIONS

1st4sport Level	What a coach will be able to do
1	Assist other more qualified coaches or work independently using UKCC National Source group resources only to deliver coaching activities
2	Have an understanding of safe, ethical and effective coaching and be able to prepare, deliver and review coaching sessions
3	Have the ability to plan, implement, analyse and revise annual coaching programmes
4	Have the ability to design, manage, implement and evaluate the process and outcome of long-term/specialist coaching programmes

Table 1 describes the skills acquired at each level of the UKCC endorsed qualifications.

Many countries throughout Europe and the rest of the world have developed their own table tennis coaching qualifications, and to find out about these contact your own table tennis association.

In addition to these, the International Table Tennis Federation (ITTF) has its own Coaching Awards, details of which can be obtained from the ITTF website.

Useful addresses and websites are given in Part 5.

The ETTA Butterfly Skills Awards

The ETTA Butterfly Skills Awards are primarily intended for the young player aged 5–16. However, they are also suitable for adults just starting to play the sport, and include adaptations for disabled players. The aim is to assist in the development of basic table tennis skills in a fun and safe environment.

The tests have been developed to monitor a player's progression and technical ability at each stage of their development.

Of course there are some advanced techniques and tactical knowledge not covered in this programme that an élite player would need to compete at the highest level of the sport. But a player who has completed these awards will have all the building blocks in place to develop their

TABLE 2: ETTA BUTTERFLY SKILLS AWARDS

Level	Equipment	Aims	Skills needed
Starter	Table tennis bats Table tennis balls Hula hoops Cones or similar Butterfly Skills Net	Test ability to control and strike a table tennis ball with a bat.	Beginner learning basic striking skills for first time. Basic hand–eye coordination, simple movement.
Improver	Table tennis bats Table tennis balls Improvised table *and* Butterfly Skills. Net OR table tennis table and net	Test ability to play basic strokes, including service, and to start developing rallies. By the time the Gold Award is achieved, the player should be capable of playing a match.	Improver who is still developing hand–eye coordination, balance and movement. Improver who has developed their striking skills.
Advanced	Table tennis bats Table tennis balls Table tennis table and net	Test ability to play more advanced strokes, using good footwork, and incorporate into basic match tactics. By the end the player will have learnt how to analyse technical and tactical aspects of table tennis.	Can play basic strokes, serve, return, and perform sidestep movement.

TABLE 3: POLYBAT SKILLS AWARDS

	Bronze	Silver	Gold
Polybat	N/A	Gaining control and direction in striking a stationary ball on a table.	Basic attacking and defensive strokes.
Starter	Grip. Balancing and bouncing the ball on the bat. Throw/strike/catch in pairs. Ready position.	Balancing and bouncing the ball on the bat with movement. Basic side-stepping movement.	Striking with forehand and backhand to targets on the floor.
Improver	Service throw. Basic forehand and backhand drive strokes. Combine backhand and forehand.	Forehand and backhand drive rallies to different targets. Basic forehand/backhand combination rally with movement.	Forehand and backhand push strokes. Basic service and return. Forehand and backhand to two targets.
Advanced	Advanced strokes.	Advanced footwork patterns and stroke combinations.	Advanced service, return and match tactics.

game as far as their talent and commitment will allow, and enable them to compete with confidence in table tennis events.

Table 2 gives an overview of the awards, including equipment required, the overall aim of the award, what skills players will learn and the skills they will need at the start of each level.

The Polybat skills awards, which are aimed at young people with severe physical impairment, are now incorporated fully into the Butterfly Skills package, so that there is a logical progression through the entire programme.

Players may enter the programme at the Bronze Award (Silver for Polybat) or whichever level is most appropriate to their age and ability.

The skills award programme is particularly useful for use in schools; two sets of lesson plans are provided, one for Key Stages 1 and 2 and one for Key Stages 3 and 4, within the programme manual. For more information contact the ETTA.

Alan Cooke stretches to block a ball on the forehand.

PART 2

SKILLS AND TECHNIQUES

CHAPTER 5

THE GRIP AND BAT ANGLES

The Grip

The first decision a player has to make is how to hold the bat. There are different grips that can be used but the important questions that you have to address are:

- What are the advantages and disadvantages of each?
- Which will best suit me?

The grip favoured by most players in the Western world is known as the 'shake hands' grip.

The Shake Hands Grip

The shake hands grip is utilized almost exclusively in Europe and with increasing popularity in Asia. The shake hands grip allows for a strong forehand and backhand but has a limited range of movement for the service. The Swedish were the first to remove the last three fingers from the bat handle during service to allow for greater wrist mobility. Thus, the service is performed with the thumb and index finger only and this is now the method utilized by all top shake hands players. Traditionally, a neutral shake hands grip has been taught which allowed for equal strength forehands and backhands and which didn't need to be changed during the rally. However, with the changing of the grip for service and greater specialization in styles, there are now a number of variations.

The bat is held in the palm of the hand as if you are shaking hands with your bat. The thumb and forefinger lie roughly parallel to the straight edge of the rubber. The remaining three fingers are wrapped loosely around the handle to provide stability. In this position, they provide fine control

over the bat. Some top class players adopt shake hands grips that favour the forehand or backhand stroke production.

Both of these have as many disadvantages as they do advantages as can be seen in Table 4.

When starting to play, and for most players, it is important to play with a neutral grip so that you get the maximum possibilities from both wings, forehand and backhand. Another point is that if you do not have a neutral grip you automatically give your opponent a lot of free information about your style of play and the stroke you are about to play.

Many of the top players change grips during the rally to effect the most mechanically efficient grip for the technique being used. Jan-Ove Waldner is the master of this technique, often deceiving opponents by cleverly altering grip, placement, spin and speed at the last possible moment.

But not all players have the ability to do this effectively and it certainly isn't an easy technique to learn.

The Penhold Grip

The development and popularity of this grip has been put down to the similarities between the grip and using chopsticks and is therefore very natural for players from many Asian countries. The thumb and forefinger circle the handle and the remaining fingers curl (as for the Chinese) or spread (as for the Japanese) on the back surface (reverse side) of the bat.

At one time, only one side of the bat was used to produce strokes from both the forehand and backhand sides of the table. This required extremely fast footwork and some weakness on the backhand, as

---

TABLE 4: TECHNICAL CONSIDERATIONS OF THE GRIP

Grip	Strength	Weakness
Neutral	Gives no information to your opponent and the maximum possibilities from both wings.	
Backhand	Good backhand block and topspin and helps the forehand topspin across the diagonal and the forehand flick.	Weak against a ball to the body and it is difficult to play a forehand topspin down the line especially against chop or a forehand topspin over the table.
Forehand	Gives more variation in forehand play and helps the topspin over table and backhand flick.	Makes the backhand topspin and backhand block against extreme topspin difficult as well as changing from forehand to backhand in an offensive situation.

the grip made it difficult to generate speed and spin. Today, however, backhands from the reverse side of the bat have been developed and are being used by penhold grip players. It is not an easy technique to master.

The penhold grip is not favoured in European countries because players in general from this region are not fast enough or light enough on their feet to play at the top level using this grip.

Grips to Avoid

Any grip which is mechanically inefficient and will limit your development as a player should be avoided. Here are some examples.

- Having the index finger in the middle or two fingers on the backhand side as both these will impede the backhand strokes.

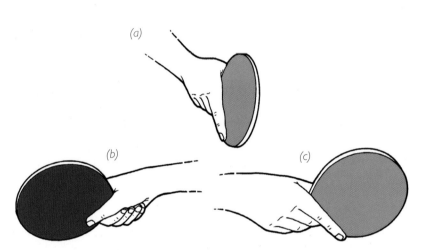

Figure 7 The shake hands grip: (a) neutral; (b) forehand; (c) backhand.

Figure 8 The penhold grip: (top) forehand; (bottom) backhand view.

- Adopting the thumb in the middle of the bat in a hammer-like grip reduces fine control.
- Gripping the handle too low down or having too high a grip on the handle as this limits movement of the wrist.

BAT ANGLES

Bat angles are very important in table tennis, as many different ones are utilized to produce the various strokes and alter the amount of spin, which will be explained in more detail later when we learn about the advanced strokes in Chapter 9.

The three basic bat angles are described as being neutral, open or closed. When the bat is held so that the head is in a vertical position, the angle is described as neutral.

When the striking surface is angled upwards, the angle is described as open and is used to produce backspin (control)

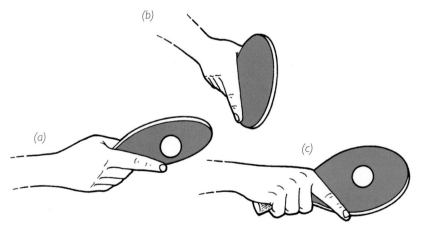

Figure 9 The basic bat angles: (a) closed (backhand); (b) neutral; (c) open (backhand).

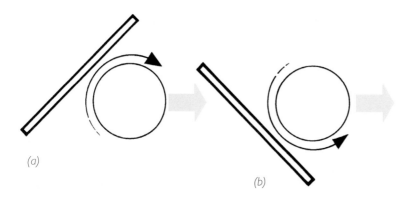

(a)

(b)

Figure 10 The bat angles, ball rotation and spin produced. (a) Closed bat angle (topspin). (b) Open bat angle (backspin).

strokes. When the striking surface is angled downwards the angle is described as closed and is used to produce attacking topspin strokes.

A closed bat angle produces topspin because it causes the ball to rotate away from the player, but an open bat angle will produce backspin because it causes the ball to rotate towards the player (see Figure 10). The degree to which the bat is 'open' or 'closed' will determine how much backspin or topspin is imparted on the ball and is a very important aspect of playing table tennis. This will be looked at in more detail in Chapter 9.

As a defensive player Joanne Parker adopts a service position further over to the forehand side of the table than would an attacker.

CHAPTER 6

THE BASIC STROKES

Introduction

The previous chapter introduced the basic bat angles used in table tennis. The important things to remember are that strokes played with open bat angles produce backspin which ensures a low bounce and is good for control, and that closed bat angles produce topspin and can be struck harder and faster as the ball is being hit in a downwards direction.

By far the majority of table tennis players throughout the world adopt an attacking style of play and even defensive players need to have a good attacking element to their game to be effective. Occasionally, attacking players are forced to use backspin strokes for control, hence the need for all players to learn all the basic strokes. The first attacking strokes to learn are the forehand and backhand drive. Both these are played with a closed bat angle. The two basic backspin strokes to learn first are the forehand and backhand push. Both these are played with an open bat angle, and provide a player with the early control they need.

The order in which these should be learnt is quite contentious with coaches, but remember the strokes you learn to rely on first will always be the ones you will revert to in a tight situation. So any player with an attacking style should start with the attacking strokes and not the control ones. For some people the control strokes are easier to learn which is why they are often the first ones taught, but my advice is don't become reliant on control strokes at the expense of the attacking ones as these will be your main weapons.

Once the basic techniques of these early strokes are mastered, then more spin and variation of spin can be added by fine adjustments of the bat angle and these will be described later.

Initially a player should just think about hitting the ball at the top of the bounce and slightly in front of the body. It is easier to achieve this if a player plays close to the table with the space between the body and the upper bat-holding arm having room for an imaginary orange and keeping the lower part of the arm relaxed. If a player prefers to play slightly further away from the table, the arm should be straighter and the space between the body and upper arm should have room for an imaginary small football.

> **TOP TIP**
>
> When starting, always try to hit the ball at the top of the bounce and slightly in front of your body rather than when the ball is to the side of your body. This will give greater success and more control, but as you improve then there are benefits in making contact with the ball to the side of the body, as you will learn later.

The Stroke Cycle

The strokes are broken down into four phases which helps to describe and analyse them (see Figure 11 overleaf):

1. Ready position
2. Backswing and preparation
3. Forward swing and contact
4. Follow through.

Ready Position

The ready position is an important base stance and can be thought of as a neutral position from which all possible strokes can be easily played. The player is in a position

watching and waiting to respond to the ball being played by his/her opponent. The feet should be shoulder-width apart (or slightly wider), knees slightly bent, body leaning slightly forward from the hips and the weight on the front part of the foot to provide balance and movement. The body should be positioned an arm's length from the table and the bat should be held in front of the body and above the table so it is easy to transfer to forehand or backhand.

Players using mostly forehand attack will have a ready position close to the backhand corner, with the left leg slightly forward for right-handers, so that the majority of balls can be played with the forehand.

Players with both forehand and backhand attacking strokes used equally, will adopt a ready position slightly left of the centre to enable attacking strokes from both forehand and backhand to be played.

Defensive players will often adopt a ready position in the centre of the table in order to cover most of the table with the forehand or backhand. A defensive player's ready position is also more square-on to the table than the attacker's, as can be seen when you compare Figures 12 and 13.

> **TOP TIP**
>
> Variations of the ready position exist according to the playing style but when starting out the ready stance adopted by forehand attackers is preferable.

Backswing

In this phase players respond to the ball played by moving their feet, the whole

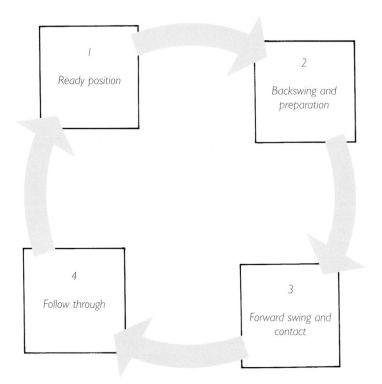

1		2
Ready position		Backswing and preparation

4		3
Follow through		Forward swing and contact

Figure 11 The stroke cycle.

body and in particular the bat arm into a position ready to produce the appropriate stroke. It is also referred to as the preparation phase.

Forward Swing and Contact

In this phase the movement of the body, the weight transfer and the forward path of the bat arm needed to make the desired contact with the ball is described. Also important here is the timing of the contact which is different for many advanced strokes but for basic strokes you should aim to make contact at the top of the bounce.

Follow Through

This phase includes the path of the bat arm after contact has been made with the ball and the body movement needed to complete the stroke and return to the ready position. A poor or shortened follow through is indicative of poor stroke production. An overly long follow through will cause problems because of the time you need to recover for the next stroke.

> **TOP TIP**
>
> To begin with, and for all the basic strokes, the point of contact should be as near to the top of the bounce as possible as this makes it easier to produce a good contact and successful stroke.

The free arm is the one not holding the bat but is very important in:

- Tracking the ball
- Balance
- Aiding upper body rotation.

The free hand is mainly used to track the ball, ensuring that the ball is taken in the same position in relation to the body each time.

Figure 12 The ready stance for an attacking player.

Figure 13 The ready stance for a defensive player.

TABLE 5: THE TWO DRIVE STROKES

Stroke cycle phase	Forehand drive	Backhand drive
Ready position	Bat arm leg slightly back or square to the line of play and close to the table.	Square to the line of play and close to the table.
Backswing	Upper body rotates 45 degrees to the right and the weight moves on to the right leg and the bat arm moves backwards and downwards at the elbow with a closed bat angle.	Bat arm moves backwards towards the waist with a slight rotation at the waist to the left.
Forward swing and contact	Path of the bat arm is forwards and upwards as the body unwinds keeping a space between bat arm and the body. Weight transfers from the right to the left leg. Contact is at the top of the bounce and in front and to the right of the body.	Forward swing is short, forwards and slightly upwards from the elbow with a closed bat angle. Contact is at the top of the bounce and slightly to the left of the middle.
Follow through	The bat edge finishes pointing in the direction of the intended play in front of the head. The player then returns to a neutral ready position.	Bat edge should finish pointing in the direction of the intended play. The player then returns to a neutral ready position.

To assist balance and upper body rotation, the angle of the free arm should be complementary to that of the bat arm. In this way it behaves like a counter-balance and aids the degree and speed of rotation.

The Two Drive Strokes

These two strokes, the forehand (FH) and backhand (BH) drive, are produced using a closed bat and therefore produce some topspin and can be developed to be played both fast and hard. The ball is hit almost at the back of the ball to begin with but because the bat angle is closed and follows through in an upward direction a little topspin may be imparted on the ball. At first the use of too much speed or power will make it harder to learn the stroke, so wait until your stroke is well grooved before trying to hit the ball too hard. These drive strokes are the basic attacking strokes from which all the advanced attacking topspin strokes are developed.

The Two Push Strokes

The forehand and backhand push strokes are used for control; they are used when the approaching ball is low and short which means it would bounce twice on your side of the table if you didn't hit it. The aim of the push strokes is to prevent an opponent from playing a powerful stroke or to force an error. This is achieved by keeping the ball as low and short or long as possible, which requires good control. Balls placed in the middle will not maintain control as these are often the easiest to attack.

Control is achieved by playing the stroke close to the body and using the elbow and wrist. For this reason the backhand push is easier than the forehand push as the latter has to be played with the bat arm further away from the body. Use of the shoulders and weight transfer is not as important as it is with the drive strokes because the strokes are played with minimal speed and power. The push strokes are the basis for all advanced backspin strokes, in which the amount of spin and length is varied

by changing the point and angle of bat on contact. They are also the basis for learning the advanced push return of service options described in Chapter 10.

When learning to play any stroke it is important that you practise directing the ball down the three major lines of play and not concentrate on just one. Many players learn to play across the diagonal first because it is easier but it is essential that you can play down the line and into the middle of the table just as accurately and effectively. The ability to out-manoeuvre an opponent by good placement of the ball on the table is a very important tactic used in table tennis. Figure 30 shows the lines of play (table placements) you should concentrate on when practising. If you and your practice partner are both right-handed this will mean that for any diagonal or middle-line placement you will both use the same stroke, but for placements down the line one will play backhand and the other forehand.

It is also very important to start combining forehand and backhand strokes in your practice as soon as you have learnt to play both drive strokes. It is less important

Figures 14–17 The stroke cycle for the forehand drive. Figure 14 Ready stance. Figure 15 Backswing and preparation. Figure 16 Forward swing. Figure 17 Follow through. *Figures 18–21 The stroke cycle for the backhand drive.* Figure 18 Backswing and preparation. Figure 19 Forward swing. movement across should be minimal. (Figures 20 and 21 opposite.)

to do this with the push strokes as you should always be looking to attack any ball that is long enough to do so, and so the use of forehand and backhand push combinations in rallies is limited. However, for any short, low balls the push stroke may be the only one you can play in order to maintain a rally. To develop control, and touch on both the forehand and the backhand, some combination work will be valuable. Obviously for a defensive player it is vital to be able to combine both push strokes and the use of push and attack.

Combining forehand and backhand strokes requires movement from side to side and so good footwork is essential and this is discussed in Chapter 8.

TOP TIP

To achieve more accurate placement, different types of targets can be used, such as paper or card shapes of different sizes, or paper cups. Alternatively, areas of the table can be covered up to make them unusable by using a towel or something similar.

Figure 20 Stroke shows the closing of the bat angle just after contact. Figure 21 The follow through is kept short and forward.

A long backswing is being used to increase the speed on contact in the service.

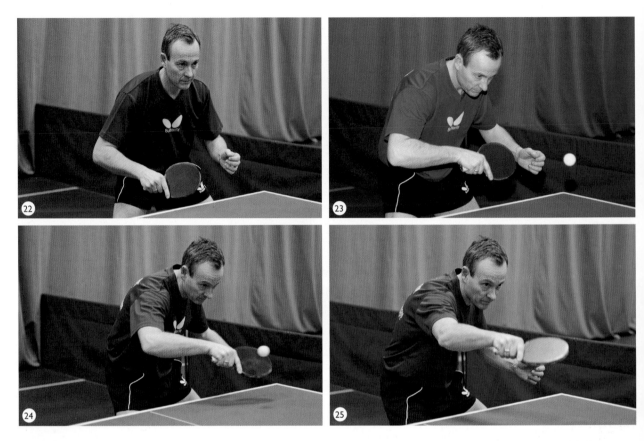

Figures 22–25 The stroke cycle for the backhand push. Figure 22 Ready stance. Figure 23 Preparation shows good tracking of the approaching ball as the bat is moved into position. Figure 24 Forward swing shows contact with the ball is made with an open bat angle. Figure 25 Follow through.

TABLE 6: THE TWO PUSH STROKES

Stroke cycle phase	Forehand push	Backhand push
Ready position	Crouched with left foot slightly forward or square on and close to the table.	Crouched with right foot slightly forward and close to the table or square on.
Backswing	Bat arm pivots back and slightly upwards from the elbow. Wrist is angled back and there is a slight rotation of the upper body.	Bat moves backwards towards stomach with an open bat angle.
Forward swing and contact	Bat arm moves forward and downwards from the elbow. Contact is made at top of the bounce underneath the ball with an open bat angle.	Stroke is produced from the elbow as the bat moves forwards and slightly downwards contacting the ball underneath at the top of the bounce.
Follow through	Bat continues to move forward and downwards. Recover to the ready position.	Bat continues to move forward and downwards. Recover to the ready position.

Figures 26–29 The stroke cycle for the forehand push. *Figure 26 Ready stance. Figure 27 Backswing and preparation. Figure 28 The forward swing and the lowering of the stance in order to make contact underneath the ball. Figure 29 Follow through.*

Joanne Parker illustrates the use of backspin (chop) when driven back from the table.

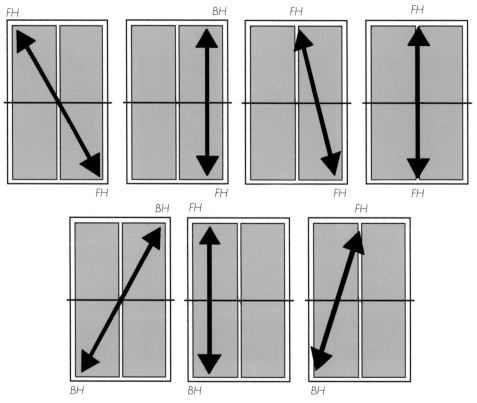

Figure 30 Table exercises to practise different placements.

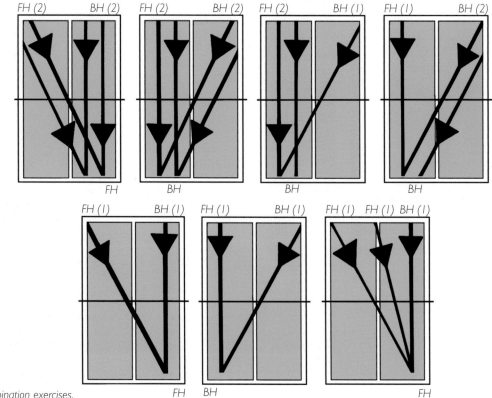

Figure 31 Combination exercises.

CHAPTER 7

THE BASIC SERVICE AND RECEIVE

The Service

To start a rally in a game a service has to be used. When first starting to learn the basic strokes it is not essential to start the practice with a service and in fact to begin with it is easier not to. However, the service technique should be learnt as soon as a player has learnt to control the ball on the table.

As you will remember, the ball has to be thrown up vertically at least 16cm (7in) from the palm of an open hand before it can be struck on the way down. This may sound easy but the co-ordination needed requires practice.

Start by just throwing the ball up from the free hand with the bat held flat so that the ball bounces on the bat as it falls. This will help to develop a good throw-up and at the same time help you get used to moving the bat towards the ball as it starts to fall. The next stage is to hit the ball on its downwards path so that it bounces on your side of the table and over the net onto your opponent's side. Both the backhand and forehand can be used for a service, but long term the forehand service will be the most important one if you are to be an attacking player; it will put you in

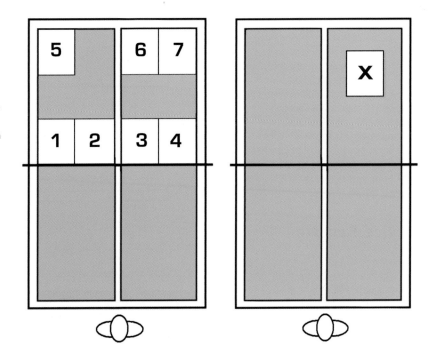

Figure 32 Service placement exercises using targets. X = moveable target. This could be a sheet of A3, which is folded after each successful 'hit' to make it harder.

TOP TIP

Basic Service Decisions

If you are trying to stop your opponent from attacking first then a short backspin service will be the better one to use, but if you want your opponent to attack then a long backspin or topspin service will serve the purpose better. Remember not to serve long to an opponent's strong side or you will be immediately at a disadvantage in the rally.

a better position to attack with the forehand which for nearly all players is their stronger side.

The angle of the bat when you first start to serve is also important. If you adopt a closed bat angle you can apply more speed and topspin, while an open bat angle will produce backspin and keep the ball lower. Both techniques are useful and need to be learnt. Try out both and see which you find easiest, but then start to think about what you are trying to achieve with the service, as it is the only time you have complete control over the ball and is therefore thought of as the most important stroke in table tennis.

When serving, the grip should be relatively loose and relaxed to allow good flexibility in the wrist in order to maintain control. To achieve a low trajectory over the net the contact point should be about 15cm (6in) higher than the surface of the table: in most cases almost immediately after the ball starts to fall following the throw-up. As you improve, an even lower contact point will allow you to increase the amount of spin on the ball more easily.

The service should be varied in length, speed and direction and again using target areas is a good way of practising this.

The length of a service is most easily varied by altering where the service bounces on the server's side of the table. When your service action has improved, you will also be able to achieve a change in length by adjusting the bat angle and contact point.

In the early stages to achieve a short service the ball needs to bounce close to the net on your side of the table, and to achieve a long service the ball needs to bounce near to your end of the table.

As you have probably realized, you don't even need a practice partner to improve your service, and the top players spend hours working on their own or with a coach to improve the placement, spin and speed of their service action.

The photos show the basic grip, ready position and throw-up action required to produce both a backhand and forehand service at the starter stage. More advanced service advice is given in Chapter 10.

Service Receive

Service return is regarded as the second most important stroke after the service because a good return by the receiver can give them control of the rally. At basic level, the player should only use two types of return based on the two different types of strokes they have so far learnt to play: the drive or push.

In preparing to return the service, the player adopts the ready position as dictated by the position of the server. The position the server takes up will dictate the possible placements they can make, so the receiver should position themselves in order to cover the possible resulting angles. This will be explained in more detail in Chapter 11 where tactics are discussed.

An attacking player should always be looking to attack a service if it is long enough and only make a push return if the service is too short or low to attack.

The receiver should be trying to vary the direction of the return by using all the available angles and lines of play. In particular, if a player is unable to attack the return decisively then the safest placement is into the body of the opponent, known

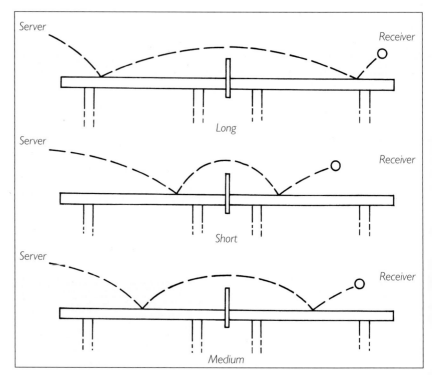

Figure 33 Diagrams to show where the ball needs to bounce to produce different length serves.

Figures 34–35 The basic backhand service action. *Figure 34 The ready position shows the right leg needs to be slightly back to allow room to make contact. Figure 35 The throw-up is made in the front and slightly to the side of the body.*

as the crossover point. The crossover point is the point on the table where a player has to make a choice of whether to play a forehand or backhand stroke and uses up time while making this decision. This hesitation often results in the player producing a weak return. As you can see in Figure 38, the crossover point is roughly in line with the right hip for a right-handed player.

Figures 36–37 The basic forehand service action. Figure 36 To enable the throw-up to be made to the side of the body the player moves side-on to the table. Figure 37 The bat moves down and forwards on contact.

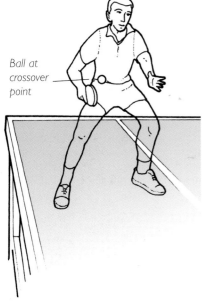

Ball at crossover point

Figure 38 The position of the ball at the crossover point.

Paul Drinkhall moves in to return a short service whilst partnering Joanne Parker in the mixed doubles at the English National Championships.

CHAPTER 8

MOVEMENT NEEDED FOR TABLE TENNIS

As with any movement from one place to another, there are specific phases that make up the whole sequence of movement; good footwork starts with the head and upper body and progresses down to the feet. If the head moves first, the body weight will follow, making the work of the legs easier. If the movement is balanced, co-ordinated and controlled then it will be more efficient and economical. In a beginner the opposite is often what happens, with the only thought being to get to the ball as quickly as possible and if some form of balance and control is maintained it has been achieved by chance.

By understanding the principles of the movement required to achieve efficient footwork you will also learn how to practise what is required. Biomechanics is the area of sport science concerned with understanding and achieving this.

The components that make up good movement from place to place are stability and balance, correct weight transfer and efficient footwork.

Stability and Balance

The ready position discussed earlier is both stable and balanced, enabling the player to move in any direction. If the feet are too close together or too wide apart then balanced movement from this position will be restricted. By ensuring the legs are bent and the weight is distributed evenly over the centre of gravity, the player is able to push off in any direction whilst maintaining balance. The centre of gravity is the point around which the body weight is balanced or centred. This is usually around the navel area.

If the player's position is too upright with minimal knee bend and the feet close

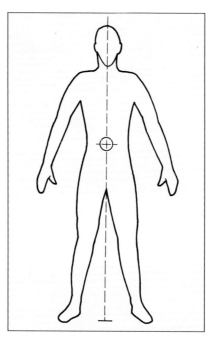

Figure 39 Centre of gravity.

together, the centre of gravity will quickly move outside the base of support.

Increasing the size of the base of support, which is the distance between the feet, increases the player's stability. Lowering the centre of gravity by bending the knees also increases stability. For most players the feet should be about shoulder-width apart until they have advanced the use of power when more rotation of the body is used and the stance will need to be wider.

In table tennis there is a combination of rotational and linear movement which brings about additional forces with which the player has to contend. The faster rotational speed needed when producing power, speed and spin will force the periphery of the body outwards from its

axis. Adjustments to the base are then required in order to maintain stability and balance, that is, by lowering and widening the stance as described above.

Transfer of Weight

Transfer of weight from one leg to the other is essential for the effective production of strokes involving any rotation. To achieve this with attacking strokes we need to have one foot slightly more forward than the other so weight can be transferred first from the front one to the back one with the backswing, and then from back foot to the front one during the forward swing in order to increase both spin and speed whilst still maintaining balance. At the same time the knee of the leg taking the weight needs to move in the direction of the rotation to finish almost in line with the foot, and at the same time the knee of the opposite leg needs to bend more and turn slightly inwards. For defensive strokes, the transfer of weight also goes from the front foot on to the back foot in the backswing, but because the forward swing goes in a downward direction weight is not transferred to the front foot in the same way that is needed for attacking strokes. The weight tends to be more evenly distributed on both feet on the follow through.

Footwork

Good footwork can provide great benefits, enabling a player to reach the ball easier and earlier so they can play a greater variety of strokes, place the ball better, deprive an opponent of time and recover more quickly whilst remaining balanced.

Good footwork achieves these benefits by ensuring you are always in position early enough to make the same correct contact and stroke, so reducing the need for any last-second adjustments.

There are different types of footwork patterns needed for table tennis, but the most used one is side-to-side. This is the type of footwork used close to the table and therefore needs to be fast and economical.

Movement to the left is started by pushing off with the right foot and the left leg moves into position with the right leg following, if necessary, so that balance is maintained. Space needs to be maintained between the feet in every step taken in order for you to be balanced when playing the stroke and to enable you to push off for the next movement.

Movement to the right is started by pushing off with the left foot, the right leg moves into position and the left leg follows.

Crossover footwork is used when a player has to cover longer distances, usually because of being further away from the table, and is very like running in order to cover the greatest amount of distance in the shortest amount of time. As a result of this movement the stroke may need to be played in a twisted position which will reduce its efficiency.

TOP TIP

Crossover footwork should not be used for short distances as it makes it difficult to make last-minute adjustments from a twisted position, and also increases the time needed to recover.

One-step footwork is used when a ball is played very quickly by an opponent and there is not enough time to get into the ideal position. It can be used to move left, right and forwards for shorter balls, or backwards for longer balls, by moving one foot away from the other into a wider stance than normal to cover the extra distance needed. This means the body position for the stroke is not optimal and

the stroke has to be played mostly with the wrist and forearm utilizing the opponent's speed and topspin. It is therefore not very effective for playing slower balls with little or no spin, and should only be needed when you have to make last-second adjustments because you have been caught off guard or misread the placement of the ball.

Players step to the left into a wide stance by pushing off with the right leg and then moving the left leg, or to move to the

right by pushing off with the left leg and moving the right leg, both creating a wider stance than normal. To enable movement forwards or backwards into a wider stance in order to reach the ball, the appropriate leg needs to be moved towards the ball in whichever direction needed, for example left and forwards.

Another movement pattern required in table tennis is the movement in for returning a short ball, and then out again into a ready position in order to attack

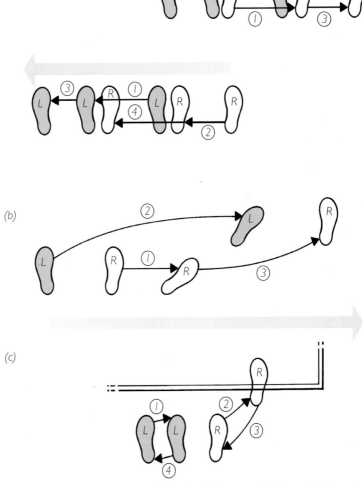

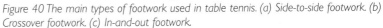

Figure 40 The main types of footwork used in table tennis. (a) Side-to-side footwork. (b) Crossover footwork. (c) In-and-out footwork.

the longer ball if it comes. This type of footwork is used quite a lot because the short service is a tactic used to stop an opponent gaining the advantage.

For right-handed players returning a short ball from anywhere other than very wide to the backhand requires the right foot to move under the table with the body angled forward and with the right arm slightly bent. After the stroke has been completed the right foot will return to the ready position.

In some cases it may be necessary for a slight side movement towards the ball before the right foot moves forward and under the table. This is to make sure you are close enough to play the return with the necessary control.

When a ball is played short and very wide to the backhand, the left foot will move forward allowing the player to recover into a position to use an attacking forehand.

Both one-step and crossover footwork can be thought of as instinctive movements and are therefore already movements that have been learnt in childhood. One-step would be used when responding to catching a ball which requires a slight movement left, right, forwards or backwards. Crossover footwork would be used naturally to move a longer distance in many situations.

Side-to-side footwork is rather more specific, as is the movement in and out required to return a short ball in table tennis. These movement patterns need to be learnt and practised in context so that they become natural. In this way a player will learn to move economically whilst maintaining stability and balance in a controlled and purposeful manner.

All the combination exercises introduced in Chapter 6 are useful for practising side-to-side footwork; Figure 41 shows more on the table exercises designed to help develop smooth economical footwork.

In-and-out footwork can be practised by a technique called multi-ball or by your practice partner serving the ball short and then playing the third ball long so that you have to move in and out.

Multi-ball is used widely in table tennis and it requires a coach or player to deliver many balls to the player like a machine to practise a particular aspect of the game. The 'feeder' may deliver the ball by throwing it or hitting the ball after bouncing it on the table from close to the net or from the end of the table, depending on which position enables the best placement for the technique to be practised. This is particularly useful in the early stages when players are not able to achieve accurate placement for each other within a rally.

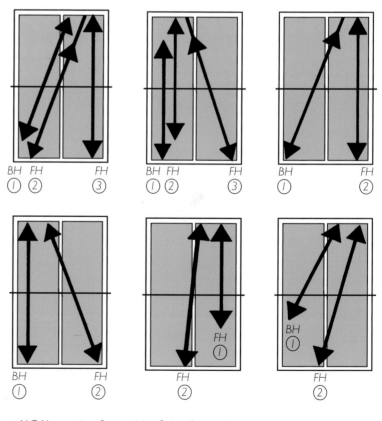

Figure 41 Table exercises for practising footwork.

CHAPTER 9

ADVANCED STROKES

Once you have learnt to play the basic strokes with confidence and developed good movement around the table, then you are ready to develop your game by learning the more advanced strokes used in table tennis.

It is at this time that you should be thinking about what style of play you want to adopt so you can concentrate on the strokes you will use most. It does not mean that you will ignore the other advanced strokes as it is important to learn how to play all the strokes to some degree. This is because although an attacking player will try to play attacking strokes whenever possible, there will be occasions when they will be forced to play more defensive strokes, such as when forced away from the table or to return a short, low, backspin ball.

Likewise a defensive player always needs to be looking to attack any weak stroke played by an opponent and therefore needs the attacking strokes in their armoury.

Advanced Attacking Strokes

All these strokes are developed from the basic forehand and backhand drive strokes, and only differ in the length of the swing, speed of the stroke and angle of the bat on contact which will dictate the amount of spin imparted.

The use of the whole body to generate power is also important. Although 'speed glue' has reduced the need for the whole body to be used to produce the same amount of impact force on contact between the bat and ball, the maximum force possible is only achieved by the use of the whole body.

With a longer swing more power can be generated but an overly long swing increases the time needed for the stroke to be played, which will in turn affect the recovery time needed. It is important, therefore, to compromise between stroke length and

power in a fast rally. Speed and spin are the important ingredients required in a fast rally and can be produced using a relatively short swing and the correct bat angle.

On the other hand, when playing an opponent who is using a lot of backspin and is away from the table, then a longer swing is feasible as you will have more time to play your stroke and will need to produce more topspin and power to counter the backspin.

There will also be occasions in the modern game when you will need to counter topspin with topspin both close and away from the table. This is a difficult technique, and to begin with it is usual for players to learn to block against topspin. From the block the counter-spin stroke can then be developed.

The bat angle and point of contact will vary depending on the spin on the ball played to you and whether you want to emphasize spin or speed with your own stroke.

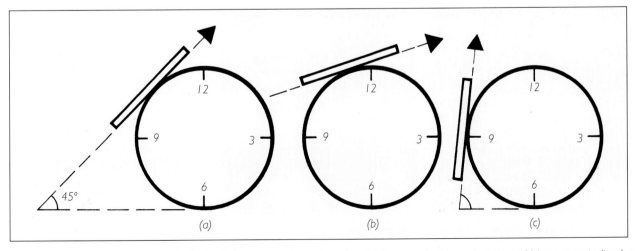

Figure 42 Contact points and bat angles for the different types of topspin strokes. (a) Fast topspin, (b) counter topspin, (c) heavy topspin (loop).

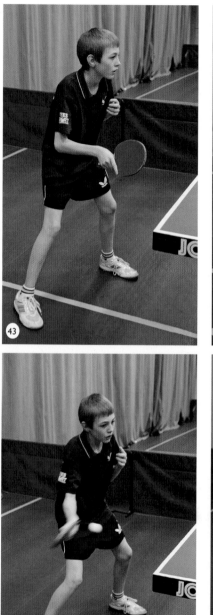

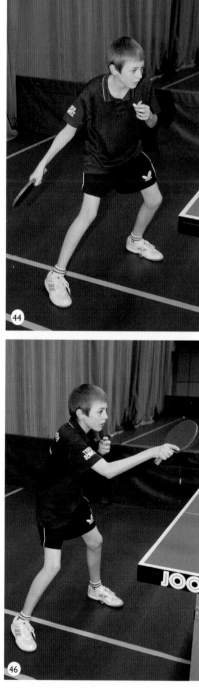

Figures 43–46 The stroke cycle for fast forehand topspin. Figure 43 Ready position. Figure 44 The backswing is longer than for the drive and there is more upper body rotation. Figure 45 The direction of the forward swing and contact almost at the side of the body. Figure 46 Follow through is forward and upwards.

In order to understand the point of contact and bat angle differences in the topspin strokes it is useful to think of the ball having a clock face (see Figure 42). Topspin involves a 'brushing action' of the ball in an upward direction between 9.30 and 12 o'clock.

The Block

The forehand and backhand blocks are variations on the drive strokes. The main differences are that the ball is struck before the top of the bounce and the length of the stroke is shorter. There is virtually no body action or follow through and the ball is returned using the spin and power imparted on it by the opponent. The spin and speed simply make the ball rebound off an almost stationary bat. The bat angle is crucial in controlling the spin and power on the ball so that the more spin there is on it the more closed the bat angle needs to be to control the rebound.

The block is considered to be a control stroke and as such could be regarded more as a defensive stroke, but some top players use it more aggressively and punch the ball back. The stroke is still very short and is punched in a forwards direction. Other top players use a 'chop block' where they move the bat downwards with a short fast movement which imparts backspin on the ball in order to counter the spin and speed.

The Fast Forehand Topspin

In this stroke the backswing is longer than for the drive and the forward swing is almost a whip-like action to produce maximum speed. The back foot is slightly further back and there is more upper body rotation than there is for the drive. The bat angle needs to be at about 45 degrees and contact on the ball is at about 10.30 and struck at the top of the bounce. At this angle the brushing action needed to impart spin is possible, unlike with the drive strokes which impart little topspin as the ball is hit almost at 9 o'clock rather than brushed. The follow through needs to

Figures 47–50 The stroke cycle for forehand topspin against backspin. *Figure 47 The player moves into a position far over on the backhand side so that the whole table can be covered using the forehand. Figure 48 In the backswing the bat is lowered and there is a lot of upper body rotation. Figure 49 In the forward swing the body unwinds and the bat brushes the ball upwards with an open bat. Figure 50 The follow through finishes at head height and the body unwinds.*

be kept fairly short to maximize recovery time for the next stroke.

The Heavy Topspin (Loop)

This stroke is used against backspin, and allows more spin to be imparted on the ball. The backswing is longer than for the fast topspin, and starts at about knee height. The forward and upward swing can be played quite quickly or slowly. The ball is brushed almost vertically in an upwards direction, making contact at about 9.30 and is struck later than top of the bounce at about table height. The path of the bat arm is almost vertical at about 85 degrees to achieve this contact, and the resulting follow through is longer than for the fast topspin. Because the player has more time to recover they are usually able to play the forehand topspin stroke from all positions on the table.

Figures 51–52 The differences with the forehand counter-spin. Figure 51 The closing of the bat angle in the backswing can be seen clearly. Figure 52 The bat angle in the forward swing remains closed and the wrist moves forward to help counter the topspin already on the ball.

The Forehand Counter-Spin

This stroke is played to counter the topspin put on the ball by an opponent by playing a topspin stroke yourself. It is developed from the 'block' by closing the angle used and brushing the ball with a longer stroke, similar to the fast topspin stroke. It can be played close to the table or a little way back from the table.

To counter the spin, the elbow needs to be kept higher than normal on the back and forward swing. The ball is brushed almost horizontally, making contact at about 12 o'clock and struck before or at the top of the bounce when playing close to the table. When this stroke is played away from the table the stroke is played with a slightly more open bat angle and after the top of the bounce as the ball begins to fall. The follow through needs to be kept quite short, in order to allow a quick recovery.

To impart more power and spin, it is essential for the body movement to be co-ordinated in order to maintain balance and stability during stroke production. With all the advanced topspin strokes a greater degree of rotation is required at the hips and waist in order to accentuate the length of the swing. To achieve this the player must push strongly from the legs from a good balanced position which may require a slightly wider stance than for the drive strokes.

Backhand Topspin Strokes

The use of the wrist is very important with all the backhand topspin strokes, as the majority of the spin and power is generated by the forearm and wrist which is why it is usually less powerful than the forehand topspin.

Against backspin the bat needs to start below the ball height and this is achieved by the starting position being between the legs at about knee height, and similar to Figure 54, but with the wrist angled downward so it can brush the ball almost vertically. The wrist then accelerates through on contact in order to get the maximum spin and speed from the brushing action. However, this stroke is rarely used because most players favour their stronger forehand topspin against backspin players. This is because they are able to play their forehand from all positions on the table because the ball comes back to them much slower from the defender who is away from the table. This was shown clearly in Figure 47 where the forehand attack against backspin is being played from the backhand side of the table.

On the other hand, the backhand fast topspin and counter-spin are widely used because in fast rallies it is not possible to use the forehand from all positions on the table.

The greater use of the wrist, and length of stroke needed, are achieved for the fast backhand topspin by moving slightly further back and allowing the stroke to start lower in front of the body (see Figures 53–56). The greater use of the wrist can also be clearly seen in this sequence of photos. There are other players that make more room for the stroke by playing it more to the side of the body, by moving their left foot (if a right-hander) slightly back and rotating at the waist more.

As already emphasized, there is a greater use of the wrist in these strokes; in the counter-spin an almost horizontal bat angle is needed to counter the topspin on the ball as the stroke is shorter than the forehand counter-spin. The wrist is crucial in succeeding to counter the topspin as it generates the extra bat speed needed to counter the topspin already on the ball and impart the counter-topspin.

Figures 53–56 The fast backhand topspin. Figure 53 The ready stance. Figure 54 Look at the greater use of the wrist in the preparation as it is pulled back. Figure 55 In the forward swing the wrist moves upwards and forwards. Figure 56 The wrist fully extends in the follow through.
Figures 57–58 The backhand counter-spin. Figure 57 In the backswing the wrist is turned backwards and downwards in front of the body. Figure 58 In the forward swing the whipping action at the elbow and wrist achieve an almost horizontal brushing action, generating the spin and speed needed to counter the topspin already on the ball.

Advanced Backspin Strokes

Backspin strokes are mainly used by defensive players. However, this term gives a false impression of the tactics they use. Good defensive players do not just rely on their opponents making mistakes but force them to make errors or weak returns by the use of deception. This deception is achieved mainly by disguising the amount of backspin on the ball by using the wrist to alter the bat angle at the point of contact.

The production of backspin requires the bat to make contact with a 'brushing action' in a downward and sometimes slightly forward direction between 8.30 and 6 o'clock on the ball.

A clock face can again be used to illustrate how bat angle and point of contact will alter the amount of spin imparted.

The Chop (Backspin Defence)

The chop is the main weapon of the defensive player and is mostly played well back from the table with backspin.

To play the forehand chop, the player starts from a ready position with the left foot slightly forward and in a balanced position to move in any direction. The player moves away from the table into position to play the ball with the right leg moving back as the elbow bends so that the bat is brought upwards to head height. The forearm and wrist move downwards and slightly forwards towards the ball, brushing underneath it at the point of contact needed to impart the desired amount of backspin. The non-playing shoulder should point in the direction the return is intended to go. The angle of the bat needed to make the desired contact is altered at the last possible moment in order to disguise the amount of backspin that will be on the ball. The point of contact is at about waist height as the ball is dropping, but height of contact will need to vary depending on the distance away from the table and the angle of the bat. Contact is made with the weight on the back foot which helps to reduce the speed on the ball. The bat continues in its forward path and the weight is transferred from the back foot to both feet into the ready position. This is shown in Figs 60–63.

The only difference with the backhand chop is that the right foot is slightly forward when moving into position to play the stroke, and the left leg moves backwards as the elbow is bent and the bat is moved up to shoulder height on the backswing. Again, the weight should be on the back foot when contact is made. The stroke cycle for the backhand chop (backspin) is shown in Figures 64 to 67 overleaf.

The Float

The defensive player uses variation of spin to outwit their opponent but they also use no spin. To achieve no spin the defensive player makes contact at about 9 o'clock with a bat angle which is almost vertical, and lightly hits the back of the ball rather than brushing it. This results in no or very little spin being imparted and often results in an opponent topspinning the ball off the end of the table in an attempt to lift the backspin that they thought was on the ball. The rest of the stroke is exactly like a chop and it is only at point of contact that the bat angle is altered in order to deceive the opponent.

Smash and Lob

The smash and lob are described together because they are strokes used against each other in a rally. They are also unusual

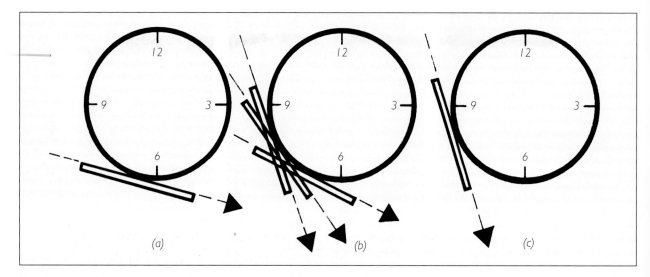

Figure 59 Bat angles and contact points for backspin strokes. (a) Heavy backspin, (b) subtle variations possible by changing the bat angle, (c) float.

Figures 60–63 The stroke cycle for forehand chop (backspin). *Figure 60 Ready stance. Figure 61 During the preparation and backswing phase the bat is moved up to head height. Figure 62 Swing is downwards and slightly forwards as the bat is moved towards the ball. Figure 63 After contact the bat follows through in the same downwards direction.* **Figures 64–67 The stroke cycle for backhand chop (backspin).** *Figure 64 Ready stance. Figure 65 The backswing is more to the side of the body than with the forehand chop. Figures 66 and 67 are overleaf.*

66

67

Figure 66 In the forward swing the bat moves downwards and forwards to brush underneath the ball to produce backspin. Figure 67 Following contact the bat follows through in the same downwards direction.

because the smash is an attacking stroke that has no topspin put on the ball, and the lob is a defensive stroke used when a player is forced away from the table and requires a lot of topspin to be imparted on the ball to be effective.

The smash is an attacking stroke used to hit the ball as hard as possible. It is used when there is no or very little spin put on the ball by their opponent, and when the ball bounces higher than normal or is played against a lob, in order to get over the height of the ball and hit it in a downwards direction. It is a stroke used to try and finish the rally but this is rarely achieved with just one smash.

The ready position for the smash requires the player to be side-on and slightly back from the table. In the backswing the arm is brought back directly behind the path of the ball with the body rotating back, transferring the weight onto the back foot.

The height of the backswing will depend on the height of the bounce. Ideally, the smash is performed at shoulder height at the top of the bounce, but sometimes the bounce is too high to do this and contact is about head height. The weight is transferred onto the front foot on the forward swing, and contact is made in front of the body. All the body weight moves forward on the follow through and the player then returns to the ready position.

The smash can also be taken early before the top of the bounce to give the opponent less time, though this is a higher-risk stroke as perfect timing is crucial to success. Another option for higher balls is to jump and make contact in the air, to enable shoulder height contact or to allow the ball to descend to shoulder height.

The lob is a defensive technique played well back from the table in

response to a smash or fast topspin that has forced you out of position and away from the table. A long topspin action which lifts the ball high in the air is used to make the return. The aim is to land the ball deep on the table with the maximum topspin so the ball bounces high and your opponent has to move away from the table to play the smash. The lob is often used when a player is out of position to give them more time to recover in order to play a more aggressive stroke on the next ball.

It is, however, quite usual to see a number of lobs played in response to smashes before the lobber can gain the upper hand again. In many such encounters, once the lobber has been forced back they often never get the opportunity to get back to the table and eventually lose the point.

In order to play the forehand lob, the player needs to adopt a forehand topspin ready position away from the table with the left foot forward. The right shoulder is then rotated backwards and downwards until the bat is at knee height. A relatively vertical brushing topspin action is used on the forward swing with contact depending on the height of the smash. Ideally contact will be about waist height but it is often higher. The bat follows through in an upward direction finishing head height.

For the backhand lob, the player first moves towards the ball and adopts a backhand ready position with the right leg and shoulder slightly forward; the bat arm moves downward and to the side of the body. The backswing takes the bat to a starting position below the height of the ball and anywhere from between the legs to the outside of the left leg in order to make space for the stroke. Again, a relatively vertical brushing topspin action is used with contact depending on the height of the smash but around waist height.

The bat follows through in an upward direction finishing about head height.

Figures 68–69 The forehand smash. *Figure 68 The player moves side-on to the table in order to make room for the smash. Figure 69 It is important that the bat starts above the ball in order to hit it downwards.*

Figures 70–72 The forehand lob. *Figure 70 The player moves towards the ball and lowers the bat in preparation for the stroke. Figure 71 Contact is made with the bat brushing upwards to impart topspin. Figure 72 The ball travels upwards and forwards and the follow through finishes with the bat about head height.*

Figures 73–75 The backhand lob. *Figure 73 The bat is lowered and the player is in position to return the ball. Figure 74 The ball has been brushed upwards and is moving upwards and forwards. Figure 75 The follow through and the ball rising due to the topspin imparted.*

CHAPTER 10

ADVANCED SERVICE AND RECEIVE

Advanced Service

The service is regarded as the most important stroke in table tennis, and once a basic short and long service has been mastered then the player needs to learn how to vary the spin, speed and direction of the ball while at the same time learning to disguise this variation. The wrist is crucial for achieving variation in the advanced service, and to ensure free movement of the wrist during the service the grip needs to be altered. The bat is held as loosely as possible by the thumb and forefinger which allows it to move like a pendulum in any direction. After serving, the other three fingers return to the handle in preparation for the next stroke.

Multiple variations can be made by varying the point of contact on the bat and ball and the direction the bat moves. Most top players using the same action and making a last-second change of the bat angle and contact point on the bat and/or ball can produce backspin, sidespin, topspin or no spin, as well as alter the placement to the forehand or backhand, short or long, fast or slow; in other words, it's 'same action, different serve'.

Disguising the service by following through in a completely different direction to the service action is also used to make

an opponent unsure as to where the contact took place and so misread the spin.

The toss can also be varied in height, which will alter the speed of the ball when contact is made by the bat: the higher the toss the faster the ball will be travelling on contact.

Forehand Sidespin Service – Left

The ready position for this service is with the ball lying on the palm of the free hand and the bat held close to the table end line in the backhand court. The feet are positioned with the right leg well back and the body in a crouched position.

For this service the ball toss is about head height and the bat is held by the thumb and forefinger with the wrist bent back towards the forearm. The bat moves back with an almost horizontal open bat angle and brushes underneath the ball to impart backspin. To impart left sidespin as well as backspin the bat will brush across and underneath the ball on the left-hand side.

If the service is combining sidespin with topspin, then the wrist is accelerated so the bat moves forward brushing the ball on the left side with the bat angled forward (closed), whereas when combining sidespin with backspin the bat is angled backwards (open).

After contact, the bat moves in the opposite direction to the ball to make it more difficult for the opponent to see where contact occurred.

Forehand Sidespin Service – Right

The service action is identical to the Forehand Sidespin Service – Left described above, except that the ball is brushed in

the opposite direction on the right-hand side which produces the opposite sidespin. It too is usually combined with backspin using an open bat angle or topspin using a closed bat angle.

Forehand High Toss Sidespin – Left or Right

The high toss service action allows the ball to generate more speed on the descent prior to contact. More spin and speed can thus be imparted to the ball. For the opponent, following the path of the high toss is more difficult and also makes it harder to watch the point of contact because of the increased speed of the ball.

From a side-on position, the ball is thrown above head height as the bat is moved into position with the wrist bent back towards the forearm. The elbow is close in to the body and the ball is contacted in exactly the same way as for the normal toss service. The angle and contact point will depend on whether it is left- or right-hand, top- or backspin that is being imparted, just the same as for a normal toss service, as explained earlier.

The bat continues in its path to the left for a short distance, then moves in the

---

KEY POINT

A service can be varied by:

- Altering the point of contact on the bat
- Altering the angle of the bat on contact with the ball
- Disguising the follow through
- Altering the height of the toss.

KEY POINT

Following the service rule change in 2002, the free arm has to be moved out of the way before the bat makes contact with the ball. Previous to this both the body and free hand were often used to shield the contact making it more difficult for an opponent to 'read' the spin that had been imparted.

Figures 76–79 The forehand backspin serve with a medium throw-up. Figure 76 The player moves side-on to the table. Figure 77 The throw-up is of medium height. Figure 78 The bat is brushing under the ball to impart backspin and the free arm is moved out of the way. Figure 79 The bat moves forward and downwards on the follow through.

opposite direction to the right to make it more difficult for the opponent to see where contact occurred.

Backhand Sidespin Service – Left or Right

The backhand service has been used increasingly following the service rule changes of September 2002, which banned a server from shielding the ball with their body in order to prevent their opponent from seeing the point of contact (see photos on page 51).

The bat starts behind the ball near the forearm. The legs are positioned with the right leg forward (though a neutral stance can also be used).

The ball toss is in front of the body; the bat and forearm are in a horizontal position.

With the body in a lowered position, contact is made on the lower left side of the ball, giving backspin and left sidespin. With the bat moving forward and underneath on the lower right side of the ball, backspin and right-hand sidespin is produced. Contacting the ball on the lower left side will produce left-hand sidespin and brushing underneath the ball will add backspin.

Changing the Contact Point on the Bat

Spin variation can also be achieved using what appears to be exactly the same action by changing the contact point on the surface of the bat. Because of the pendulum action, if contact is made at a point near the handle, the bat is moving more slowly than at a point near the bottom edge of the bat. The greater the speed the greater the spin will be, but the action appears to be exactly the same to the opponent standing at the other end of the table.

In backspin serves, the same variation can be achieved by making contact near to the leading part or the back part of the bat surface. In this case the bat at the leading point will be moving the fastest, so more spin will be imparted if contact is made

Figures 80–83 The forehand sidespin or backspin service using a medium height throw-up.
Figure 80 The ready position is low and side-on to the table. Figure 81 The bat moves back towards the stomach in preparation for the forward swing. Figure 82 Contact is made in front of the body and the bat brushes sideways and underneath the ball. Figure 83 The player completes the follow through, trying not to give any clues as to where it will bounce.

here. Again it is very difficult for an opponent to see this difference (see Figure 88).

Use of the Long Service

Long services are mostly used as a variation to the short serve. It is a big advantage if the service action is basically the same, no matter whether you intend to produce a short or a long service. The surprise factor is more than 50 per cent of the difficulty caused in returning a long service. All the different services described earlier can just as easily be produced long, but will be more effective if they are both long and fast.

To produce a long, fast service the bounce needs to be near the server's end of the table, and the contact point has to be at about net height otherwise the serve will be too high.

The 'kicker serve' is a popular long service that imparts strong topspin and is best used in combination with short backspin and no-spin serves, all with the same action. The kicker service involves, at the last possible moment, changing the bat angle to approximately 45° forward and using a 'mini topspin' action with the wrist. This causes the ball to 'kick' off the table often catching your opponent by surprise. Variation is achieved by making contact along the path the bat moves, which is first into the waist area and out again (resembling the shape of a banana) and is sometimes referred to as a 'banana serve'.

Return of Service

It is important to watch the contact of the bat with the ball as this is the best way to observe what spin is on it. The angle of the bat will also indicate if the serve is backspin, no-spin or topspin. The direction of the bat movement at contact indicates whether the serve has left or right sidespin. To counter sidespin it is necessary to put the opposite spin on the ball to that put on by the server. Both the direction of the bat and the angle of the bat are the best indications of the spin, so the server will try to disguise these as much as possible.

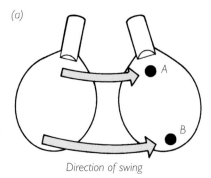

(a)

Direction of swing

(b)

Direction of swing

Figure 88 The speed effect of different contact points on the bat for (a) pendulum action and (b) backspin action. For both actions the bat will be moving faster at point B than at point A.

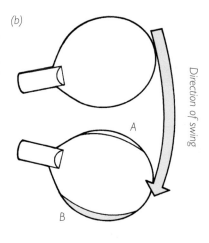

Long serves should always be returned with topspin by attacking players, and most defensive players will also attack a long service as a surprise tactic or to gain the initiative.

Short serves can be returned using a flick, long push or short push.

As with the service, you do not want to give clues about which return you are going to use so to disguise your return you need all three to start with a similar initial movement. Then and only at the last moment the angle of the bat is altered in order to flick, long push or short push with variation of the placement. In this way, like the serve, the opponent will only have the minimum amount of time to react to the return.

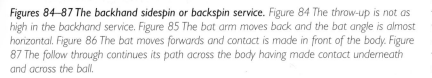

Figures 84–87 The backhand sidespin or backspin service. Figure 84 The throw-up is not as high in the backhand service. Figure 85 The bat arm moves back and the bat angle is almost horizontal. Figure 86 The bat moves forwards and contact is made in front of the body. Figure 87 The follow through continues its path across the body having made contact underneath and across the ball.

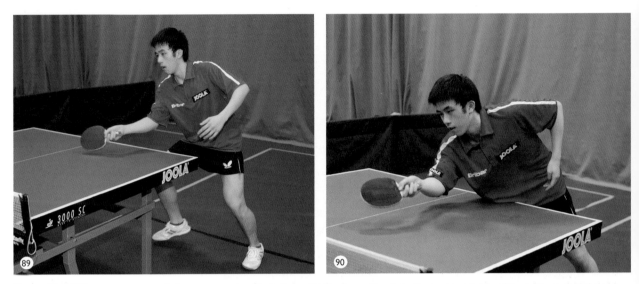

Figures 89–90 The movement needed to return a short ball. Figure 89 Ready position is to the backhand side of the table so that the player can attack any long service with the forehand. He has started to move in having anticipated it will be short. Figure 90 The player moves the right foot under the table and transfers his body weight forward, which allows the elbow to remain bent in order to maintain control.

Good footwork is vital when returning short services otherwise you will find yourself unable to recover quickly enough for the next stroke. The head needs to be as close to the contact point as possible and if you do not move in close enough to the ball the arm becomes too straight resulting in loss of control (so do not stretch for the ball, move towards it.)

To avoid stretching, the foot nearest the ball moves under the table with the body angled forward and the arm slightly bent. For a short ball played to most areas of the table, this will be the right foot for right-handed players. Only when the ball is very wide will the left foot be the best one to move forward. The wrist is used to

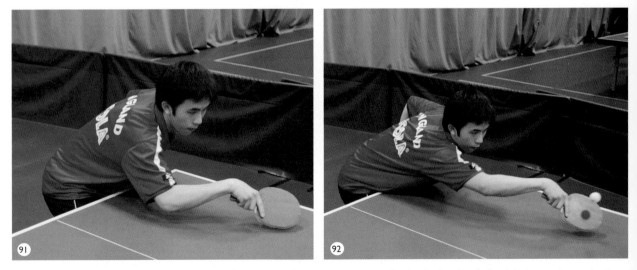

Figures 91–92 The backhand touch return. Figure 91 The same forward movement as for the forehand, with the right leg moving under the table. The bat angle is open so as to impart backspin. A last-second change of angle could be made to impart float. Figure 92 The follow through after contact. The open bat angle tells you that backspin has been imparted on the ball.

control the length of the ball and to impart the required spin.

After contact the player recovers by moving the right leg back into the ready position for the next stroke.

The Short Push Return

A short return limits your opponent's attacking options and is used in order to gain control and to restrict your opponent's decision time. The wrist is used to brush the ball underneath and produce backspin, thus making it more difficult for your opponent to attack. As already explained, in order to get close enough to the ball the right leg moves under the table for right-handers with the body angled forward and the arm slightly bent. The forearm moves forward and the bat contacts the ball at the top of the bounce or just before, with an open bat angle and brushing action achieved by a last-moment adjustment of the wrist. The player then returns to the ready position ready to play the next stroke.

However, a variation with no spin ('float') can be used, as this can result in your opponent misreading the spin and

giving you a high return. In order to put no spin on the ball, contact is on the back of the ball with little or no brushing action. In order to disguise this, the follow through needs to look the same as if you have brushed under the ball with an open bat.

The Attacking Push Return

To play this stroke the receiver should move towards the short ball in the same way as for the short touch return and the bat angle and contact alteration should be made at the last possible moment so as to disguise the length.

This stroke is performed usually with backspin, although no spin can be used as a variation, but is not an easy stroke and if anticipated by your opponent can be attacked more easily. The long push is taken early or at the top of the bounce. It needs to be played quick, and deep into the crossover point, or wide which will force your opponent to move. It is a return used by both attackers and defenders so that the server has very little time to play a strong attacking stroke and you have the opportunity to gain the advantage.

The Flick Return

The movement used is the same as for any short return. Adjustments to the bat angle and contact are made as late as possible so that the server does not know which return you are going to use.

The flick is an attacking stroke played either with the forehand or backhand against a short ball, using mostly the wrist and forearm. The flick is produced by using an upward, brushing action against backspin, while the bat angle needs to be more 'closed' against no spin, sidespin or topspin. A fast action will also minimize the effect of the opponent's spin. Quick recovery is essential as the follow through over the table leaves the player in a vulnerable position.

Figures 93 and 94 show the forehand flick and Figures 95 and 96 the backhand flick return.

The right leg moves under the table for right-handers towards the bounce of the ball with the body angled forward and the arm slightly bent at the elbow. Contact is made at the top of the bounce in front of the body with the elbow as the pivot point. The stroke is performed with the forearm and wrist brushing the ball upwards using different

Figures 93–94 The forehand flick return. Figure 93 The neutral angle of the bat as the player moves forward again with the right foot. Figure 94 The player close enough to the ball on contact to maintain a slightly bent elbow.

Figures 95–96 The backhand flick return. Figure 95 The neutral angle of the bat on approach. Figure 96 Look how the wrist flicks over on the follow through.

closed bat angles depending on the spin on the ball.

The player then recovers by moving the right leg back into the ready position.

The greater use of the wrist with the backhand flick is clearly seen in Figure 96 as the wrist literally 'flicks' over following contact.

Analysis of Strokes

As you develop your strokes it is important to be able to learn what is good about them and what needs improving. It is difficult to do this for yourself and the best person to help is a coach, who will be more able to identify the causes of any weaknesses and set you the best table exercises to make improvement.

However, if you don't have a coach available you should ask a team member or practice partner to give you feedback using a form similar to the one in Table 7. The use of more in-depth analysis will be introduced in Chapter 12.

TABLE 7: STROKE ANALYSIS TEMPLATE

Stroke	OK	Not OK	What's wrong?
Ready position			
Backswing			
Forward swing			
Contact and bat angle			
Follow through			
Use of whole body			

PART 3

TACTICS

CHAPTER II

GENERAL TACTICS

Basic tactics are used to force an error or weak shot from your opponent in order to win the point. The use of deception is important in table tennis tactics and this is achieved by variation of spin, speed and placement at every stage of a rally starting with the service.

Any tactic has to build on the player's technical ability. In other words there is always a connection between technique and tactic. A good technique will give you many more tactical possibilities because you will have a greater repertoire of strokes to rely on.

Having a good tactical awareness is vital in table tennis and it is important that you understand what you are trying to achieve with a particular tactic, and that it is based on what you perceive the weaknesses and strengths of your opponent to be. If you have never played this opponent before you will need to analyse the player as you begin to play the match and adjust your tactics in response to what you learn as the match proceeds. If you have played this opponent before then you should already have some idea of his or her weaknesses. It's always a good idea to make notes about a player's strengths and weaknesses so you can be prepared for when you next play them.

TOP TIP

A well-developed repertoire of strokes will give you many tactical possibilities. A poorer technique or repertoire will restrict your options.

Understanding the effects of playing a particular stroke to a specific place on the table is the start but then come the questions about the options your opponent has, and how they may respond. To understand the responses that are possible you will need to take into account the strengths of your opponent and also plan and practise your own tactics. By practising different tactics that suit your style of play you will learn what the possible outcomes to them will be. This will help with your decision making and reduce your decision time. Your response to a given tactic will become instinctive. Because table tennis is such a fast game this is very important; the Chinese have been quoted with describing the game 'as like playing chess at 100mph'.

KEY POINT

Remember that if you stick to your best tactic all the time you will make it obvious to your opponent what you are trying to do and make it easier for him or her to read your game and so counter your tactic.

It is therefore important to vary the speed, placement and spin in different situations, so that your opponent will have to change their game.

A good tactician is someone who knows when to change tactics without losing the initiative.

Tactics need to be practised just as much as technique once you have got to a reasonable level, and at the top level it is tactics that often make the difference between who wins or loses. Tactics are best practised in match conditions and this is why competition is a vital element in a player's development. The time spent on training and competition, in terms of percentages, changes as a player develops, starting in the early stages with more time spent on training and less on competition until at the top level when the reverse is desirable.

Placement Tactics

Good placement is effective as a tactic because it exploits any weaknesses in movement that your opponent may have. These weaknesses could be one or more of the following:

- Movement to a wide ball
- Movement away from a ball to make space for a stroke
- Ability to change direction quickly enough
- Movement in and out.

The difficulty many players have is not so much with moving towards a ball but with moving away from it in order to make space to play a stroke. This is why playing a ball into the crossover point is so effective.

KEY POINT

The crossover point is the area in which the player has to choose whether to play a forehand or backhand stroke. For a right-handed player this is roughly in line with the right hip, as shown in Figure 38 on page 35.

Learning to read the play and possible placements requires practice and improves by using irregular practices. It is this type of exercise that helps to improve your anticipation and reduce the time you need for decision making. To read the play in a rally you need to look for cues from your opponent's ready stance, body movements and especially the racket arm and angle of the bat. You also have to learn to watch the flight and path of the ball.

An understanding of the possible target areas that can be played from a particular ready position on the table is also helpful in anticipating the likely placement of the ball that your opponent may use. Figure 97 shows the possible target areas relative to where the ball is being played from.

The different placements that are used will now be discussed in relation to what they are used for and what they may achieve.

1 Playing Down the Line

About 80 per cent of strokes played in a rally are placed across the diagonal because it is easier to play across the diagonal than to play down the line. The first reason for this is that the natural body rotation at the waist lends itself to diagonal play and a player needs to turn more at the waist and 'open' the shoulders in order to provide the room needed to play down the line.

Another reason for it being easier to play a shot across the diagonal is that the path is longer than down the line. This is explained by applying Pythagoras' theorem (see Figure 98). The length of a line ball can be 9 feet (3m) maximum whereas a diagonal one can be up to 10 feet 3 inches (3.3m).

By playing down the line you will therefore be doing something unexpected and give your opponent less time to recover for the next stroke because the ball is travelling over a shorter distance. A backhand attacking stroke down the line is particularly effective in this respect, because not only is the ball being played over a shorter distance but also the length of the backhand stroke is shorter than the forehand attacking stroke which your opponent will have to use against this tactic if he or she is a right-handed player. It is one of the few times the backhand attack can overcome the forehand attack because your opponent has less time to recover than you do.

2 Switching the Line of Play

This tactic utilizes the element of surprise and is particularly effective when the switch is down the line for the reasons already mentioned. Against another right-handed player, such a switch is used when you have been playing across the diagonal with your backhand to your opponent's backhand and then change to playing the ball down the line.

You could also switch the ball down the line following a series of forehand attacking strokes played across the diagonal, which can also be a useful tactic.

Any time your opponent has to react to a change of direction and move may lead

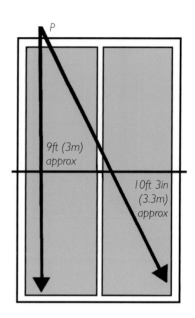

Figure 98 Pythagoras' theorem illustrating that line balls are shorter than diagonal ones.

to him or her being driven out of position or force him or her to play a weaker stroke.

In order to gain time the best counter-tactic against a switch is for your opponent to 'switch the switch'. In other words after you have changed the line of play your opponent does the same, forcing you to move from one side of the table to the other. By making you move, your opponent has gained vital recovery time for the next stroke and may even regain the initiative (see Figures 99 and 100 overleaf). You should bear this in mind.

3 Exploiting the Crossover Point

As we saw earlier, one of the most difficult movements in table tennis is moving away from the ball; any ball played into the crossover point makes a player have to do this as well as make a decision about whether to play a forehand or a backhand stroke.

One of the best tactics to exploit this area is to first play the ball wide and then play it into the crossover point. Four

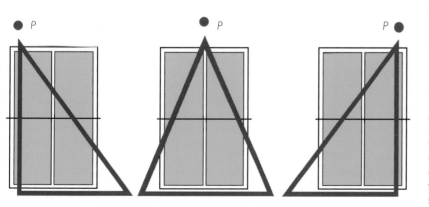

Figure 97 The possible target areas from different positions on the table. P denotes where the ball is being played from.

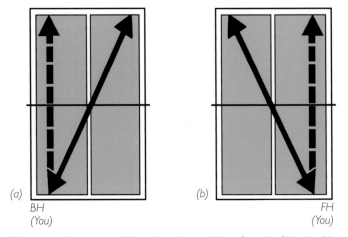

(a)
BH
(You)

(b)
FH
(You)

Figure 99 Basic switching tactics: (a) switching down the line from the BH side; (b) switching down the line from the FH side. The dotted line shows the switch.

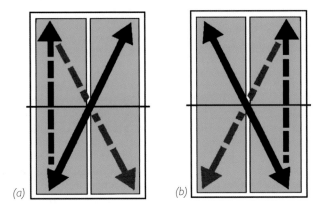

(a)

(b)

Figure 100 The use of the counter-switch: (a) switching the BH switch; (b) switching the FH switch. The red dotted line shows the counter-switch in each diagram.

different ways of achieving this are shown in Figure 101 opposite.

Just as effective is to first play the ball short and then long into the crossover point. Particularly effective is to bring the player in for a short ball near the middle of the table, and then attack into the crossover point as this will result in a lot of movement by your opponent in order to make the room needed to play the next stroke. Fig 102 shows the different exercises you can use to practise this tactic.

4 Continually Changing the Line of Play

The object with this tactic is to wrong-foot your opponent by making them change direction a number of times in a rally in order to break their rhythm. The expected outcome of this tactic is that your opponent will either make an error or a weak return from which you can win the point.

The change of direction must not be regular in any way otherwise you will help your opponent to gain a rhythm rather than disrupt it. One way of achieving your aim is to play a different number of balls on different lines (see Figure 103).

One effect of moving an opponent wide is that they may move too far and over run the ball, which will result in a weaker stroke being played as they will not be in the correct position to play a good one and may even have to play an improvised one.

Another useful change in the line of play is to use a short service to bring your opponent in on one side of the table and then force him or her back wide on the other.

5 Changing the Length

This is a tactic mainly played when a player is away from the table or following a short service. It is particularly used against a defensive player to break up their rhythm and to try and force a weak return that can be attacked. The movement in and out is quite difficult particularly if a short ball is followed by a long, fast attacking stroke.

The stroke used to place it short against a defensive player is similar to the short push but is often called a drop shot. The drop shot is then followed up with an attacking stroke directed at the crossover point or on the opposite line to the one the defender has moved in on, as this makes it more difficult for them to recover.

All these placement tactics need to be practised and they are best practised using irregular–free exercises in which there is no set sequence and the player does not know where the opponent's ball is going after the initial play; for example when practising switch tactics the practice becomes 'free' after the switch has been made, which means the ball can then be played anywhere. More information about on-the-table exercises can be found in Chapter 15.

This 'free' element helps players develop tactical awareness and improves their ability to anticipate where a ball is going to be played. All the table diagrams in this

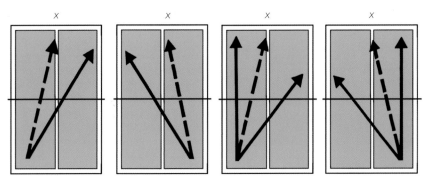

Figure 101 Table exercises to practise attacking the crossover point (shown by ×) following a wide ball.

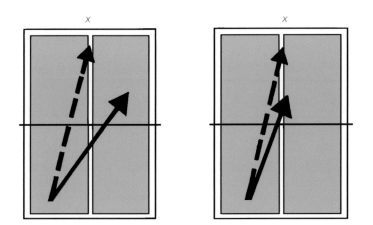

Figure 102 Table exercises to practise attacking the crossover point (shown by ×) following a short ball.

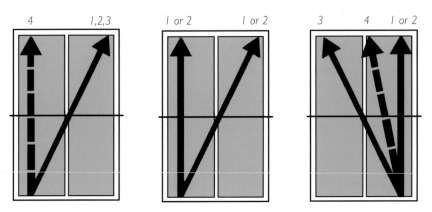

Figure 103 Table exercise for practising playing a different number of balls to different places on the table.

section can be used as a start point for irregular–free training and tactical practice (see Figs 99–103).

Spin and Speed Tactics

Variation of spin and speed in a rally is used regularly as a tactic in table tennis to deceive an opponent and force a weak stroke or error. The importance of using disguise and variation has already been mentioned in relation to the various strokes and its importance as a tactic cannot be emphasized enough.

The contact point and angle of the bat determines the spin imparted on the ball which in turn affects the path of the ball through the air (the arc) and the bounce on the table. The type and amount of spin will also affect how the ball rebounds off the bat, which in turn influences the stroke that can be played next.

The higher the impact force the faster the ball will travel; the more joints and muscles involved in stroke production the greater the force, which is known as a summation of forces. The use of 'speed glue' reduces the need to use as many joints and muscles to achieve a similar amount of impact force and has enabled players to use shorter strokes, thus making the recovery time needed less and the game even faster.

The variation of spin and speed used in table tennis will be specifically discussed in the next chapter in relation to the tactics needed and used by or against different styles of play.

Service Tactics

One of the beauties of table tennis is that the game is not totally reliant on power and can be greatly influenced by using the right tactics. As we have already seen, it is important to use variation, so that your opponent finds it difficult to predict your tactics as the game develops. The amount of variation that can be used is particularly highlighted with the service, as this is the only time in a point that you have total control over the ball.

TABLE 8: THIRD BALL 'SET PIECES'

Service	Return	Third ball
Short to the forehand	FH flick or long push to: 1 FH 2 BH 3 crossover Short touch return to FH or BH	Topspin attack to: 1 FH 2 BH 3 crossover Flick or long push return as above
Short to the backhand	Backhand flick or long push to: 1 FH 2 BH 3 crossover Short touch return to FH or BH	Topspin attack to: 1 FH 2 BH 3 crossover Flick or long push return as above
Short anywhere	Flick or long push to: 1 FH 2 BH 3 crossover Short touch return to FH or BH	Topspin attack to: 1 FH 2 BH 3 crossover Flick or long push return as above

BH, backhand; FH, forehand.

Some players tend to plan whole matches around 'set pieces' in which they start with a particular service and expect a particular return so they can use a predetermined follow-up (third ball). This can be restrictive if used too often as the tactic will become too obvious but can be very effective when used at the right time especially when it is least expected or at a crucial stage in the game. A number of players have only a few 'set pieces' or 'set services' that they use only at crucial times, such as deuce. This helps them both to keep their nerve at this crucial time and to play decisively.

The possible spin variation on the service is endless but is only really effective if it is well disguised.

Try to read the difficulties your opponent has at returning different types of spin. The decision of where to serve will depend on the opponent's quality of return on either the forehand or backhand.

If they prefer to use the forehand, they often have a good forehand flick and are good from the middle of the table. If so, it is better to serve short into the backhand or wide to the forehand. If they prefer the backhand return, then you should vary the placement between forehand, middle and backhand, so that they do not know which to prepare for. At the highest level it is important to be able to serve short with topspin or no spin, because many players, when the service is too short to attack with topspin, try to return short which is more difficult to achieve against these kinds of spin. In this way you may even force your opponent to play long.

A well-disguised short float service is worth gambling with particularly when the game is tight, such as at deuce, because at this point in a game your opponent is more likely to play the safer push return. This will result in a higher return, which will make it easier for you to attack decisively. The Olympic and World Champion from Sweden, Jan-Ove Waldner, was a great exponent of this tactic and it often proved to be the match winner.

Sometimes a half long service allows you to play a more aggressive third ball attack because it is difficult to return this length of service short. However, if you don't disguise the service well your opponent will be able to attack it and gain the initiative themselves.

It is also important not to be afraid to serve long and fast to break up a pattern of short serves so that your opponent cannot risk moving too early by assuming it will be short.

The service is an individual skill and the tactical elements need to be well practised, so that they do not collapse under pressure. It is also important to experiment with different services in order to develop your own repertoire of 'favourite' services and follow-up tactics.

The forehand sidespin service is one of the most widely used by attackers because the starting position in the backhand corner puts you in a good position to play your forehand from almost anywhere on the table. To be able to serve down the line to the right-hander it is important that you make contact with the ball at about 30cm (12in) from the corner of the table and as low as possible to keep the bounce flat (see Figure 78).

TOP TIP

A well-developed repertoire of strokes and services will give you many tactical possibilities. A poorer technique or smaller repertoire will restrict your options.

It is important not to get too obsessed with tactics, however, otherwise you will find it difficult to play your natural game and stay relaxed. By systematically practising your tactics they will become more natural.

TOP TIP

When a service bounces high on your opponent's side the most usual cause is that you are making contact too high. The lower the contact the flatter the bounce will be and the harder it is for your opponent to attack. A lower point of contact also allows you to use more spin and speed whilst maintaining control.

The use of disguise, different types of spin (top, back, no spin, left or right), speed and length on the service alone will give you a varied repertoire from which you can develop more. So get experimenting and practising.

Return of Service Tactics

If the service is the most important stroke, then receive of service must be equally important otherwise you will always lose to a player with 'good' serves.

As mentioned before, you should always try to attack half long and long services. This will often force your opponent to serve short, which gives you the possibility to vary between making short or long returns.

In order to return a short service, you need to move in and out by moving the right leg under the table so as to get as close to the ball as possible. This enables you to work with a bent arm and ensures that you are able to use both the forearm and wrist to their maximum.

Once you have moved in close enough to the short service then you have three alternative returns you can use: short or long push or flick. Variation in the return of services is just as important as it is to vary the service. It is important that your opponent does not know if the ball will be short, long or which stroke you are going to use. If both you and your opponent want to attack at the start of the rally then a short serve may need to be returned short until you can put your opponent under pressure with an attacking stroke. The goal with the short push return is to play the ball short with different amounts of spin on and to take the ball early with either the forehand or backhand so that you reduce the time your opponent has to react.

The long return should vary between using long attacking pushes and flicks. It is important to vary the placement of the first attack but it is just as important to vary spin and speed. A fast, long return is good against players who are not as strong

in attack, as it will force them to play a weak attacking stroke which you can then attack yourself.

The goal with any return is to put your opponent under time pressure so the stroke has to be made as early as possible. For all short, sidespin, no-spin and topspin serves, a player must learn to attack these with a flick, which requires more acceleration in the forearm and wrist. The flick can also be used against backspin – but the bat arm movement is more upwards and forwards. The use of a strong, deep flick will force your opponent back on their heels thus giving you the initiative.

The long attacking push technique is almost the same as a short push return, but you need to use the forearm more to get greater depth and speed on the ball. This gives your opponent less time to play a good third ball attack, and in the same way as the flick, provides you with the opportunity to be aggressive on the fourth ball.

TOP TIP

When practising the long push return, remember that the speed and the contact point should be at the top of the bounce or earlier, and that it is important to be accurate with the placement of long returns otherwise your opponent will be able to attack them and gain the advantage.

It is essential to practise the three types of return and to concentrate on being able to achieve 'good' placement so that you are able to return the service to different places on the table. The third ball 'set pieces' in Table 8 can just as easily be used to practise your returns as your services.

As with the service, all the possible variations should be practised regularly until you decide on your favourite returns and learn what the 'outcomes' will be. Your favourites should then be practised more but the others should not be neglected completely (they too may be needed on occasions for extra variation).

Doubles Tactics

In doubles, as we have already seen, each player in a pair has to play the ball alternatively and the service order changes every two points which makes it very difficult to work out the tactics to use. However, the first thing to do is to try to identify the weaker player in your opponents. This will normally be the woman in mixed doubles but may be more difficult to decide in same-sex doubles.

Once you have identified the weaker player, then your first tactical decision should be to play your 'worst' order first, so that if the match goes to a deciding game you will finish with your 'best' order.

There are some very successful pairings who prefer to play their 'best' order first so that they get off to a good start in the deciding game but the majority prefer 'worst' order first.

TOP TIP

Often the order of play can be the deciding factor in who wins a doubles match if the two pairs are similar in ability. So decide on which tactic you prefer: to use 'best' or 'worst' order first.

Remember your 'worst' order in doubles is when the stronger player in the opposing pair plays to the weaker player in your pair.

An added complication in doubles is when one of the pair is a left-hander. This can be a great advantage because the left-hander can receive service with the forehand by standing around the side of the table and still recover easily. This makes attacking short services with a flick much easier and also leaves the whole table free for his or her partner. Even when the right-hander is returning service, the left-hander is in a better position to move into any position on the table in order to play the next stroke.

A left and right combination also allows both players more space when serving as well as in the rally. The natural position they take up enables both players to use their forehands more easily than two right-

Figures 104–105 *The ready positions when receiving the service in doubles for a pair with one left- and one right-handed player.* Figure 104 *The ready position when the left-hander is receiving shows just how close they can be to any short service used.* Figure 105 *The ready position when the right-hander is receiving shows how easy it will be for the left-hander to move in for the next ball.*

or two left-handed players. This allows them to attack with stronger forehand strokes making them the most dangerous opponents. For similar reasons a player with a strong backhand is also an advantage in a doubles pairing because it allows the other player more space to use their forehand attack.

When the left-hander is returning service they have the added advantage of being able to get very close to any short service (see Figure 104).

When two right-handed players get into their ready position for receiving, you can see that they are more in each other's way to play the next stroke, making recovery

Figure 106 *The ready position when receiving in doubles for two right-handed players shows the limited space for movement in and out especially when trying to use their forehands.*

and movement in and out more difficult. Good footwork is essential.

There are also the same space – and footwork – saving benefits in having one left-hander and one right-hander when serving. The two players do not impede one another in any way and movement in and out to return the ball is much easier (see Figures 107–109). When the left-hander is serving, the right-hander has plenty of room to move in and when the right-hander is serving, the left-hander is able to stand clear of the server in a position that allows easy movement in to use their forehand.

When two right-handers are serving (see Figure 109) the server has to move right and further back to give their partner enough space to move in and use their forehand from anywhere on the table.

So the difficulties in deciding on the best tactics in doubles are caused by the complications of service changes, order of play and player positioning. However, there are some basic tactics that can be applied.

First, a short service will prevent fast attacking returns but if they are too short they will allow your opponents to exploit the angles with their return because they can move in closer to the ball more easily than in singles, because they do not have to recover straight away for the next stroke. That is their partner's responsibility.

Figures 107–108 The ready position when serving in doubles for a pair with one left- and one right-handed player. Figure 107 The ready position when the left-hander is serving again illustrates the space his partner has to move in for the next stroke. Figure 108 The ready position when the right-hander is serving.

This is particularly advantageous for the left-hander.

Second, concentrate on using backspin serves with a variation of no-spin serves for deception in order to make it as difficult as possible for your opponents to attack the service. However, the use of too much sidespin can be a disadvantage in doubles play as it is your partner to whom it will be angled back and not you.

Third, try to return short services short to the forehand. This will crowd your opponents, as the non-serving player has to move in front of the server to return the ball.

In the rally, attack into the body of the opponent who has just played the ball as this will require speedy footwork for them to get out of the way in order for their partner to have enough time to move into position to play the next stroke. Alternatively, play the ball fast and long into the crossover point of the incoming player so

Figure 109 The ready position when serving in doubles for two right-handed players shows the difficulties of moving out of each other's way.

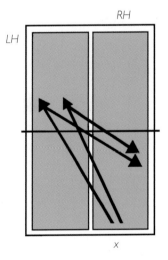

Figure 110 This shows how the angle of a short return can be maximized in doubles because the player is closer to the ball on the return of service, especially the left-hander. x indicates the server.

TOP TIP

Always make sure your partner knows what service you are going to use so that they have a better idea what return is likely to be made. This is usually achieved by using agreed signals under the table so that your opponents can't see them but your partner can.

that they have to make last-second adjustments to their movement.

Doubles play is very challenging and helps players with their footwork, recovery and anticipation skills in particular. However, doubles practice is often neglected in training sessions. The author's opinion is that doubles should form part of any table tennis player's training programme as it offers an alternative way of developing a overall tactical appreciation and technical ability. What's more, it is good to play as part of a team rather than as an individual all the time as it gives you a different perspective. Some players perform better in doubles because they don't want to let their partner down or they benefit from the experience of the other player. Whatever the reason, doubles can be both an educational and enjoyable challenge.

Kelly Sibley shows the importance of upper body rotation in producing power in the forehand topspin.

CHAPTER 12

DIFFERENT PLAYING STYLES

Analysing Your Opponent

No two players are alike but most players can be placed into one or more categories such as blockers, choppers, penholders, loopers, left-handers and combination bat players. It is important to understand the strengths and weaknesses of these different styles of play so that you know which of the general tactics are most suitable to try against them.

Try to find out as much as possible before you play them, and the best way to do this is by watching them play. If this is not possible, then you will have to analyse your opponent whilst you are actually playing against them. Understanding the strengths and weaknesses of their style of play will help you to know what to look for and should help you decide on your best tactics early in the game. In this section each style of play will be studied in respect to the general weaknesses and strengths they possess, the tactics to try against them and the tactics they may use against you.

It's always a good idea to keep a simple record of the matches you play by asking yourself: what tactics worked well, how most points were won or lost, which service and return was most effective and what you think you should try next time. If you find this difficult to do for yourself, ask a team member to sit and watch you play and feedback this information to you after the match.

If you have a coach, then they will automatically do this for you probably using a form similar to the one in Figure 111. This form provides information on technical, tactical, psychological and physiological elements of a player's performance and can be used for analysing an opponent

PLAYER ANALYSIS TEMPLATE FOR USE IN MATCHES		
Sport specific	Rating 1–5	Comments/Advice
1. Psychological		
• Stayed focused even when things went wrong		
• Maintained concentration		
2. Technical		
• Use of service placement and variation of spin		
• Service return		
• Use of main attacking strokes		
• Use of control strokes		
3. Physical		
• Balance and agility		
• Speed of movement		
• Footwork		
• Use of the whole body		
4. Tactical		
• Dominated play		
• Maintained tactics		
• Played positively		
• Exploited weaknesses		

Tactics that worked: _____

Where I lost points: _____
_____

What I should work on for next time: _____
_____

Figure 111 Player analysis template.

or your own performance. As you can see this type of analysis exercise is more in-depth than the stroke analysis template introduced in Chapter 10.

Loopers (Topspin Players)

The 'loop' can be regarded as the topspin stroke more often played against backspin, and is usually a longer stroke than the faster topspin adopted mainly against other attacking players. It is called the 'loop' because of the loftier (looping) trajectory over the net, which results from the ball being brushed upwards almost vertically. A fast topspin has a lower, flatter trajectory because of the more acute angle of the bat on contact.

The 'looper' will always be looking for a long ball to attack because this allows him or her the chance to let the ball drop, so they can brush it upwards with a longer stroke. A long ball is classed as any ball when the second bounce will be off the end of the table.

A long ball played with backspin on makes it easier for you to impart the greatest topspin on the ball, so a good tactic for the looper is to force their opponent to push long. Two ways this can be achieved are to use a half long backspin service or pushing short when returning the service.

The opening topspin is best played into the crossover point or wide to the forehand so that your opponent has to move into position for whichever return they choose to play. This also makes it more difficult for them to use the backhand block which is the easiest stroke to use against heavy topspin for most players. Most importantly, the opening topspin needs to be strong.

A strong topspin can be one played very fast which is aimed at winning the point outright or forcing your opponent onto the back foot, but if it doesn't it will be returned to you fast. Alternatively, it could be played with more spin, longer and slower (a loop) which may result in your opponent being forced to make a return that is higher and slower, which can

then be followed up with a faster attacking stroke. A deep, slower, heavily spun 'loop' can be particularly effective against another topspin player who likes to play fast because it breaks up their natural rhythm.

Loopers in the past have tended to have quite long strokes in order to impart the heavy spin required which made them vulnerable to the ball being taken early and played fast. Speed glue has enabled the strokes to become shorter with similar effect, so this tactic is less effective against the modern topspin player using 'speed glue'.

One of the most intriguing tactical battles in table tennis is when a looper (topspin) player plays against a chopper (backspin player). Such a contest is in many people's opinion the most interesting from a spectator's viewpoint, with one player close to the table attacking and the other playing away from the table.

The Looper Versus the Chopper

The terms 'looper' and 'chopper' are still widely used, which is why I have used them here.

In the men's game it is particularly difficult to succeed at the top level as a chopper, as male topspin players often have too much power, spin and speed in their repertoire of strokes. In the women's game it is still an effective style to develop unless pitted against the very fast Asian women players who take the ball so early that the backspin hardly has time to take effect.

Nearly all defensive players rely on rhythm by playing at a speed that suits them and then getting their opponent to play at this rhythm. To prevent this, the attacker must change tactics and not be predictable. The defender will certainly vary the spin, placement and speed in an attempt to outwit their opponent and the attacker must do likewise. Some of the tactics used against a defender are to use the drop shot to move the player in and out to catch them out of position, or to use variation in spin, speed or good placement to force an error or weak stroke from them. The attacker needs to

be looking for the float (no spin) as this gives them an opportunity to attack the ball more decisively. However, if they don't spot the float it will often result in an error on their part. The float is deliberately used by the defender to force the attacker into topspinning the ball off the end of the table by fooling them into thinking it had backspin on.

Use any one of the tactics mentioned above on its own and the attacker will surely lose, because the defender will nearly always be more consistent and with good footwork can 'glide' in and out against the drop shot or move quickly to any change of direction. Defensive players are also more patient and have extremely good attacks which they will use to punish any weak shots played by their opponent, especially a drop shot played too long or too high.

The 'looper' has to use a good variation of spin, speed and placement in order to beat a defensive player, which is why it is such an interesting battle to watch. In the men's game at world-class level the attacker will usually win and, as already mentioned, in the women's game at the highest level this is even more likely. Below world-class level a defensive style of play can still be very successful.

> **TOP TIP**
>
> It is vital that the attacker changes their 'best' tactic as soon as they feel the defender is getting into a rhythm, even at the expense of losing the point. A combination of tactics will be necessary to outwit the consistent and cunning defensive player (chopper).

Combination Bat Players

A combination bat consists of a blade covered with different types of sponge and/or rubber on either side of the bat. Prior to 1984 this caused opponents a lot of problems because the combination bat player was very adept at 'twiddling' and both sides of the blade were covered with the same colour rubber. Twiddling was when the player rotated the bat round in their hand so that they could play each shot with a different side of the blade and hence different sponge and rubber. As a result of this the opponent had little idea what spin or speed to expect and had to constantly adjust their stroke at the last possible moment.

Since 1984 one side of the blade has had to have a red matt covering and the other a black one. At least with the introduction of this rule it means an opponent can see which side is being used and will know what type of sponge and rubber is being used. At the start of the match you will see the players looking at an opponent's bat to check what rubber and sponge is on each side.

However, it is still very difficult and messy to play against the combi-bat player (or 'funny' bat player as they are sometimes referred to). This is because they will continually change the side of the bat during play in order to confuse an opponent and reduce the amount of time they have to make a decision about what spin is on the ball.

If one side of the bat has long pimples then the reaction of the rubber is even more unpredictable but there are some general responses you can expect and these are shown in Table 9.

One effective tactic is to drive the combi-bat (or 'funny' bat) player away from the table as the effects of the spin will be reduced, because it 'dies' over time. This tactic also gives you more time to see which side of the bat is being used and hence which type of rubber. It also gives you more time to adjust to the spin. The flight of the ball will also help you decide what spin there is on the ball.

Another tactic that works against both 'long pimples' and 'anti-spin' rubber is to use less spin and speed yourself. Both these rubbers are classed as 'parasitic rubbers' because they gain their effects by feeding off the spin and speed imparted on the ball by an opponent.

Long serves or long, slow drives with little or no topspin on make it difficult for the combi-bat player to play a very

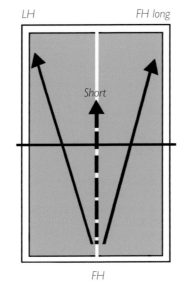

Figure 112 This exercise shows how to drive your opponent away from the table, using a long, wide ball, followed by a short ball.

effective return. As a result you are likely to receive a 'nothing' ball which can be attacked more easily. This can be even more effective if you can play a slightly shorter, slower ball with little spin when the combi-bat player is away from the table. However, if you play this tactic when the player is close to the table you will be punished, as your opponent will be able to attack and gain control again.

Blockers

A 'blocker' will mirror your speed and spin by allowing the ball to rebound back off the block stroke on either the backhand or forehand side, but will always be looking to attack any weak stroke. Blockers are usually very consistent and play the angles with great precision, which means your footwork and stamina will be greatly tested as the 'blocker' will be constantly trying to out-manoeuvre you.

The worst thing you can do is to play the lines or wide balls unless your opponent is 'out of position', because the 'blocker' will use any ball played to either wing to give you back an even wider angled ball. You will just end up having to cover more and more ground until you are worn down and start to play weak strokes.

One tactic is to spin the ball high and deep to the middle of the table to reduce the angle available to the 'blocker' and to give them very little speed to feed off. A good long ball will also force the 'blocker' back from the table a little where they are less effective. After a few of these strokes a quick switch to either wing will give you the advantage. However, if this slow, high ball is not played long enough the 'blocker' will attack it and gain the advantage, and if you don't make a good switch they will use the angle against you again.

If you can consistently play the ball long it may also force a shorter return, which is best attacked into the crossover point.

TABLE 9: POINTS TO REMEMBER WHEN PLAYING AGAINST LONG PIMPLES

Action	Effect
1. Push using reversed rubber	If returned with a push using long pimples the return will have slight topspin or no spin instead of the expected backspin.
2. Topspin using reversed rubber	If returned with a chop using long pimples it will always have backspin on the ball. The faster the initial topspin the heavier the chop will be.
3. Topspin or drive using long pimples	The ball will travel slower than with normal rubber and will have some backspin on the ball rather than the expected topspin.

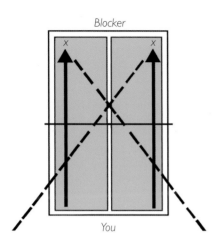

Figure 113 How a 'blocker' utilizes the widest possible angles to make you move.

This is particularly effective if you first play the ball to one area of the table, which will limit the angles that can be played against you and will also allow you to know where to recover to after each stroke. After a few strokes to this area the switch wide or into the crossover point will be all the more effective.

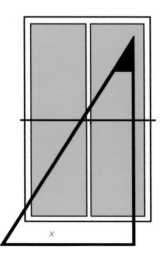

Figure 114 How to reduce the angle a blocker can use against you by playing the ball to one area of the table.

You must bear in mind that blockers use relatively short strokes most of the time, which enable them to use the switch tactic very effectively against you. Equally they will try to use consistently long returns in order to force you back from the table and force a shorter return from you, which they will then attack.

Penholders

To play with the penhold grip a player has to be very fast on their feet and have excellent footwork in order to play forehands from all angles. The Asian players who favour this grip always have very speedy and efficient footwork.

The backhand side is traditionally regarded as the weaker wing of the penhold player. However, it is second nature for them to play particularly strong forehands from the backhand side. The grip itself encourages this because the bat angle naturally faces the opponent's diagonal allowing them to play good forehand strokes from this position.

To try and expose their backhand wing the best tactic is to switch the ball wide to the forehand, which will leave a gap on the backhand wing for you to attack. The unexpected switch will often have the effect of driving the penholder away from the table, which will make it easier for you to attack into the weaker backhand.

The penhold player will often respond by switching the switch and playing you wide to the forehand, which makes it more difficult for you to get a good angle to attack into the backhand side. Figures 50 and 51 show how you can practise this tactic.

In the 1980s and 1990s this backhand weakness was exploited by the Europeans and especially the Swedish players, which resulted in a decline in the number of penhold players for a while.

With the greater use now of the reverse side attack on the backhand side by the penhold player, this tactic of exposing the backhand has become less effective. Although this stroke is technically very difficult to master it can be very effective if the covering on this side of the bat is different from that used on the forehand side.

Some penhold players have developed a very awkward reverse drive block, which they use from the backhand side and which bounces very low and fast.

Even more successfully, others such as Ma Lin and Wang Hao from China developed a reverse backhand topspin stroke in the first decade of the millennium, which made their backhands just as effective as the backhand of players using the 'shake hand' grip. The former weakness of the penhold grip player on the backhand side was reduced for these players, which is one reason why they have been so successful. This innovation also resulted in an increase in the number of penhold players once more.

Left-Handed Players

Traditionally, left-handed players have strong forehands and weaker but often quite consistent backhands. Out of

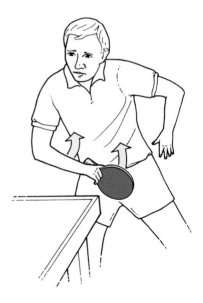

Figure 115 How the penhold reverse backhand is used to produce topspin. The three fingers bent over on the reverse side can clearly be seen. The arrows indicate the direction the bat and forearm move, achieved by rapid movement at the wrist and elbow.

necessity their forehand stroke from the backhand and middle are usually strong, but trying to cover their weaker backhand in this way does leave a gap wide to the forehand.

A good tactic therefore is to play a fast spinning ball wide to the forehand in an attempt to force a weaker return, which can then be attacked into the backhand of the left-handed player. Alternatively, the backhand can be exposed by using a fast backhand switch across the diagonal, so that the left-hander has to move wide to the forehand, and then follow this with an even faster ball down the line into the left-hander's backhand.

The obvious counter-tactic for the left-hander would be to switch the switch to your forehand down the line with their forehand in order to gain time by making you move. However, this will put you into an even stronger position

on the table to angle the ball wide into the backhand. On the other hand, your opponent will have gained valuable time by making you move to the line ball and may provide the time needed to recover position in order to protect the weaker backhand side again. The outcome of this tactical battle will depend on who plays the better-disguised switch or who anticipates it the best.

As we saw earlier, the decision-making side of table tennis is indeed like 'chess being played at 100mph'.

TOP TIP

Try out different tactics so that you learn what the possible reactions to your initial action may be. In this way you will also learn which tactics suit your style of play and don't be afraid to be innovative with your tactics. Last but not least always be willing to change your tactics. The best match-players are the ones who recognize the need to change, if only for a few points.

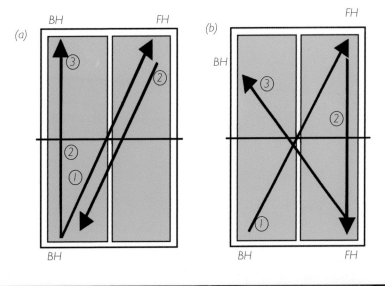

Figure 116 The use of the switch tactic against a left-hander shows: (a) how it could expose the backhand side by switching wide to the forehand; (b) the possible counter-switch the left-hander may use but the backhand will still be exposed unless he recovers quickly.

Gavin Evans plays a strong forehand topspin from a very wide position.

PART 4

FITNESS
AND TRAINING

CHAPTER 13

PROVIDING THE ENERGY

In order to get the most out of your training and competition you need first of all to understand how the body supplies the energy required to achieve the necessary movements.

Performing any activity requires muscles to contract and in order for this to happen the body must be able to provide energy. Energy for exercise, growth and repair is stored in a chemical compound known as adenosine triphosphate (ATP). There are different ways the body makes and uses ATP and these are known as the energy systems. For short bursts of energy the system provides ATP without the use of oxygen. For longer continual exercise of over 3 minutes' duration oxygen is required.

The Energy Systems

Anaerobic Systems

1. When a muscle is stimulated to contract immediate energy is obtained from stored ATP but this is quickly used up and must be replenished by the breakdown of phosphocreatine (PC). For this reason this system is known as the phosphagen (ATP-PC) and it can provide energy for up to 10 seconds without the use of oxygen. It is also referred to as the alactic energy system because it does not involve the production of lactate.
2. If the activity continues for longer than 10 seconds then more ATP must be obtained rapidly from the breakdown of glucose or glycogen without the use of oxygen. This system is less efficient than the phosphagen (ATP-PC) system but can be used to maintain high intensity activity for longer periods of 30–120 seconds. It is referred to as the lactic system because the chemical reactions include the breakdown of glucose or glycogen to pyruvic and lactic acid, which accumulate in the blood and muscles. This build up of lactic acid will limit muscle contraction and ultimately lead to exhaustion.

Aerobic System

This system is slower than the anaerobic systems because it produces ATP from glucose and glycogen via a number of complex reactions. It is, however, much more efficient and produces about 13 times more ATP than that produced by the anaerobic system. It is slower because it is reliant on oxygen being delivered to

This side-on view shows the space needed to make a good forehand service.

The ready position in doubles for two right-handed players.

the working muscles by the cardio-respiratory system.

The fitness of this system is therefore very important to the ability of an athlete to perform at their best because supplying oxygen to the muscles is crucial.

Energy from this system can be used for prolonged medium to low intensity activity. The only constraint is the supply of nutrients and if the stores of carbohydrates in the form of glucose or glycogen should be depleted, then this system is able to produce ATP from fats, the secondary source of energy in the body, and proteins.

Fats are stored as fatty acids and triglycerides in muscle and adipose cells and although they are a richer source of energy than carbohydrates, they are needed for many other functions in the body, which prevent them from being used as the primary source of energy.

Long-distance runners and especially marathon runners will utilize this source of energy and in extreme cases may use protein as a source of energy. This is a last resort as far as the body is concerned because proteins are not stored in the body and tissue cells would need to be broken down in order to supply energy.

Oxygen Uptake

Without a good supply of oxygen the aerobic energy system cannot function efficiently. The amount of oxygen consumed in a given time, usually a minute, is expressed as VO_2. The peak rate of oxygen consumption is the VO_2 max; this is the difference between the volume of oxygen inspired and expired and is known as an athlete's aerobic capacity.

Comparing VO_2 max values recorded throughout a training programme can give you an indication of the improvement being made. Trained athletes have a much higher VO_2 max than untrained individuals, which enables them to exercise aerobically for much longer periods.

Providing Fuel for Energy

As explained earlier, energy is essential for muscle contraction and this energy is stored in the chemical ATP, which is produced from our food. A well-balanced diet is essential for healthy living and even more important for any athlete, like a table tennis player, to fuel training and competitive play.

Essential Nutrients

The essential nutrients are carbohydrates, fats, protein, fluid (water), vitamins and minerals. Fibre is an additional requirement as it aids the functioning of the digestive tract and protects against a number of diseases. Fibre does not provide any nutrients as it is made up of large chemicals that cannot be broken down because we lack the enzymes to do so. Their main effect is that they provide bulk to our food, which helps everything move through the digestive system better.

- **Carbohydrates** These are the primary source of energy and can be grouped as complex ones such as starch found in pulses, cereals, bread, potatoes, pasta, rice and many root vegetables, and simple ones such as sugars found in fruit, honey and fizzy drinks. Chemically both groups are composed of carbon, hydrogen and oxygen. Complex carbohydrates are absorbed more slowly than simple carbohydrates because they are larger molecules and contain fibre. Simple carbohydrates are absorbed quickly and produce a rapid rise in blood glucose. Complex carbohydrates are a richer source of glucose, which is stored and used to produce ATP.

  Glucose is stored in the body in the form of a complex carbohydrate molecule called glycogen and is also found in the blood. The main glycogen store is in the liver but smaller stores are also found in the muscles. It is stored glucose that is normally used to provide ATP as the blood glucose is needed for other functions. Any excess glucose in the blood will be taken up and stored as glycogen in the liver.

- **Fats** Fats have a number of functions in the body but are the secondary source of energy. Fats can be either saturated or unsaturated. Saturated fats are mostly obtained from animals and found in meat, butter, cheese, whole milk, lard, ice-cream and chocolate. Unsaturated fats are obtained from plants, such as olive, sunflower oils, nuts and some margarines. Unsaturated fats protect against heart disease but saturated fat increases blood cholesterol and therefore promotes heart disease.

- **Protein** Proteins have even more functions than fats in the body but for the athlete the most important ones are the growth of cells including muscle cells, the production of enzymes essential for all chemical reactions in the body, including those in the production of ATP, and the production of hormones.

  Proteins are chemically different from carbohydrates and fats because although they all contain carbon, hydrogen and oxygen, proteins also contain nitrogen and some contain sulphur and iron. They are made in plants and animals from amino acids. Any excess amino acids in the blood will be broken down and stored as glycogen or fat. In this form they can be utilized in the production of energy.

  Proteins are obtained from animals in the form of meat, fish, poultry, eggs, milk and cheese and from plant sources such as beans, pulses, seeds and nuts.

- **Fluids** Water represents 40–70 per cent of total body mass and is essential for all chemical reactions in the body. Under normal conditions the body maintains a balance between fluid intake and output. To maintain water balance, the average person with a sedentary lifestyle should drink between 2 and 3 litres of water a day.

  However, contracting muscles generate a great deal of heat (up to 100 times more than resting muscles) and this extra heat has to be removed from the body or the core body temperature will rise to dangerous levels. This is achieved by the blood transporting the heat to the skin where it is lost through convection, radiation and evaporation (sweating). Vigorous activity produces profuse sweating which can result in fluid loss of 4–5 per cent of body mass. In these circumstances water will be lost from all parts of the body and there will be a reduction in blood volume. Less blood results in reduced cardiac output, which in turn reduces the delivery of nutrients and oxygen to the cells. The circulatory system tries to maintain blood flow to muscles by reducing flow to the skin, but this results in less heat being lost and the body temperature rises.

- **Vitamins and minerals** Vitamins fall into two groups, the fat soluble (A, D, E and K) and the water soluble (B complex and C). The most important minerals are calcium (important for bone strength and formation), iron (a component of haemoglobin and muscle myoglobin), sodium, potassium and magnesium (all important for fluid balance and production of nerve impulses). Iodine is also important for the thyroid gland and metabolism.

  Nutritional requirements will depend on age, size, levels of activity and metabolism but provided you a have a balanced diet there should not normally be any reason to take supplements unless a deficiency is diagnosed.

KEY INFORMATION

Carbohydrate intake should be approximately 7–10g per kg of body weight (approx 0.35oz per 2.2lb); 1g yields about 4.0 Kcals of energy.

Fat intake should be less than 30 per cent of dietary intake, of which 70–75 per cent should be unsaturated fats; 1g yields 9.0 Kcals of energy.

Protein intake should be approximately 1–2g per kg of body weight (approx 0.04oz per 2.2lb) and yields 4.0 Kcals of energy.

CHAPTER 14

FITNESS TRAINING FOR TABLE TENNIS

Improving fitness requires improving the physiological function of various body systems. To achieve this improved fitness, the body needs to work harder than normal by overloading the systems through exercises that progressively become more demanding as fitness improves.

The systems adapt in response to this overload and become more efficient. When this happens the overload must increase to bring about further improvement until the desired level of fitness is achieved.

An analysis of the demands of table tennis match-play illustrates the need to sustain bouts of work of variable intensities over prolonged periods, often with short rest intervals. Table tennis is predominantly aerobic with intermittent bouts of anaerobic work and all the energy systems are constantly being used to differing degrees to meet the demands of match-play.

As you have already learnt, one of the key objectives in table tennis is to move the opponent around the table in order to open up areas that they are unable to cover or to force a weaker stroke either through lack of speed, agility or fatigue. Players must be able to perform unpredictable multi-directional movements at various speeds and with frequent changes in intensity. As a result adapted stances are sometimes necessary as are extreme body positions and joint ranges particularly around the hips, pelvis and lower back.

Table tennis therefore requires a multi-component approach to physical conditioning; those components of fitness required for table tennis are summarized in Figure 117.

Agility endurance is needed to be able to reproduce the required multi-directional movements for sustained periods, and in part is developed by speed and agility drills or on-the-table exercises. The ability to control movement through a large range is achieved in part through stretching work in core strength and flexibility training. Endurance training is necessary in order to repeat back-to-back high intensity performances for the duration of a tournament.

The energy systems were described in the previous chapter. Later in this chapter you will learn how these systems are made more efficient through training.

Age Considerations of Training

The long-term athlete development (LTAD) model for table tennis, available from the ETTA, provides guidelines for physical training throughout a player's career, with close attention paid to the young developing athlete.

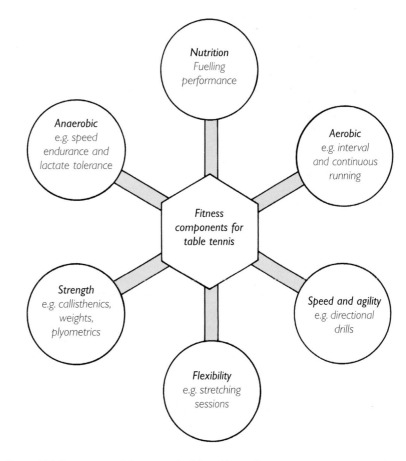

Figure 117 Components of fitness required for table tennis.

The LTAD model identifies key periods (or 'windows of adaptation') for maximizing the potential gains in different components of physical fitness as young athletes mature. The physical conditioning of young athletes must aim to maximize the development of these components of fitness during these periods and care must be taken not to introduce strength training, in particular, too early in a child's physical development. This does not mean that these are the only types of conditioning that the athlete employs during these 'windows', but that they take a more prominent role within the overall programme.

The first 'speed window' is in the 'Learning to play and train' period for table tennis which is at about 8–12 years old. During the early part of this period aerobic capacity and flexibility should be developed through fun games, and strength can be developed through activities working against their own body weight, or using a medicine or Swiss ball. The development of the ABCs (agility, balance and co-ordination) is very important at this stage and table tennis activities, particularly the early 'off-the-table' ones, can be very usefully employed to achieve these skills.

In the next LTAD period 'Learning to train' (at about age 12–16) strength training can be introduced in sessions of no longer than 30 minutes, two or three times a week. The second 'speed window' is also in this stage, and speed work should concentrate on reaction speed, short sprints, acceleration and agility. Specific stretching sessions for developing flexibility, and non-weight bearing endurance sessions to develop aerobic capacity, should also become part of the training.

At the age of about 16 table tennis players are fully trainable in all components of fitness training and it will be the individual's strengths and weaknesses that will determine training priorities and programmes from here on.

Nutritional Training

Both training and performance (match-play) need fuelling in order to provide the energy required to perform at your best. Nutritional training is vital to make sure enough of the right foods are available at the right time to provide the energy needed for training sessions and competitive play. It is essential that the body receives the correct fuel at the correct time to supply the energy needed.

What you eat on a daily basis is extremely important for both training and competitive play: your diet can affect how fast and how well you progress. Ensure all-round good eating habits and focus on your '24/7 nutrition' and not just pre-, during and post-game nutrition.

By training yourself to eat the right foods at the right time, however, you can achieve better performances both in training sessions and competition. The 'right' foods for you may be very different from those for anyone else, so you will need to keep a record of what you eat and how you feel at different stages of a competition and training session in order to find the 'right' eating programme for yourself.

Competition requires you to find out about what and when to eat: pre-competition, during an event and post-competition. The timing and content will be

Andrew Rushton moves round the table on the backhand side to play a powerful forehand topspin.

individual to your own requirements and food tolerances in these different situations. It is therefore important to experiment during full-day training sessions, first to find out what suits you best at different times and then to try this out at an event.

There are some general guidelines to help you make these decisions but a sports nutritionist will be able to advise you in more detail than is possible here, and devise an individual programme for you.

Pre-Competition

In the week leading up to an event ensure a high intake of complex carbohydrates, in particular rice and pasta as they contain more carbohydrate than potatoes. In between meals include a carbohydrate-based snack, examples of which are given in Table 10.

Also drink plenty of water the day before an event.

During an Event

Take a meal about 2–3 hours before your first match in order to top up blood glucose levels after a night's rest. The meal should not be too large and should be high in complex carbohydrates and low in fat, because fat speeds up digestion and you will not sustain the benefits long enough into the event.

It is also important to take on fluids, so drink two cups of water 2 hours before and another one about 15–30 minutes before your first match. In matches lasting more than 20 minutes it is important to take on more fluids.

TABLE 10: SUITABLE CARBO-RICH SNACKS

Small cans of fruit

Bananas

Fruit bread or fruit buns

Low-fat cereal bars

Plain biscuits or crackers

Rice cakes (topped with jam, honey or banana)

Low-fat rice pudding

Jam or honey sandwiches

Plain boiled rice or pasta with a little tomato sauce

'In-between snacks' should be eaten during any break of 1–2 hours and the carbo-rich snacks listed in Table 10 are most suitable. Try to take a supply of these with you to a training session or competition, as they may not be available at the venue.

Post-Competition

This period is very important and the goals are to refuel liver and muscle glycogen stores, provide protein to repair and grow the adapting muscle cells and re-hydrate the body by replacing the water and electrolytes lost through sweating.

The consumption of a carbo-rich snack (50g/2oz) will restore the glycogen levels and if this is combined with a snack containing protein (10–20g/½–1oz), muscle protein synthesis will be promoted for the growth and repair of muscle cells.

Recording your weight before and after competition or a training session will give an indication of how much water has been lost and how much needs to be replaced. For every 1kg lost, 1 litre of water should be drunk.

Drinking water alone may not be enough to re-hydrate the body, as the electrolyte (salts) balance must also be considered. Sports drinks are continually being developed, and contain sodium, other electrolytes and/or glucose polymer,

which is easily digested and can help to delay glycogen depletion. There are three types of sports drinks: hypotonic, isotonic and hypertonic, and they differ in the concentration of solutes in the solution. In table tennis nearly all matches will last less than an hour so the most appropriate sports drink would be a hypotonic one. This type has the lowest concentration of solutes and water is just as suitable (although some players may prefer the taste of a sports drink). However, training sessions last much longer than a match and a sports drink containing a higher concentration of solutes may be more beneficial.

Fitness Training

Warm up and Cool down

All training and competitive play needs to be preceded by a warm up. The aims of a warm up are to increase core body temperature and heart rate, and warm up the muscles and associated tissues. It will help you operate better because a warm up helps to prepare you mentally as well as make you less prone to injury.

A warm up should start with general body exercises such as light jogging, side-stepping or skipping which should slowly be increased in intensity but should not include any bounding. This light warm up should be followed by static stretching exercises covering the whole body:

- neck and shoulders (any neck movements should be slow and controlled and bending the head backwards should be avoided)

- lower back and abdomen
- buttocks, groin and hips
- front and back of thigh
- lower leg and ankle.

Static stretching as part of a warm up for children under 12 does not help to prevent injury and is therefore not necessary.

Simulation exercises using stroke play and related movements may also be added, for example shadow play. The warm up should last about 15 minutes. Most of the top players have a set warm up that they always use pre-competition, and a different one pre-training.

A cool down jog should be gentle and rhythmic, followed by stretching exercises to relax the muscles after continuous contraction during the session. The cool down should last at least 5 minutes and aim to help you relax, return your heart rate to a normal resting level and avoid stiffness and soreness in the muscles.

Anaerobic Training

There are two types of session used in anaerobic training: one for speed endurance and the other for the development of lactate tolerance.

Interval running programmes are used to develop both these in table tennis; the two types only differ in the length of the recovery time used between runs. During the recovery period you need to remain active by walking or jogging very slowly.

To develop speed endurance the recovery period is related to the time the run takes so that the lactic waste built up by the alactic system can be removed from the muscles before the next run. For instance, a sprint of 100m at 100 per cent effort would require a recovery period of two times the time taken to run the 100m at a work ratio of 1:2. However, when starting to build up your anaerobic power you may need to start with a lower work rate, depending on how fit you are, for example 1:4 where the recovery time is four times the length of time the run takes.

As you get closer to a major tournament, interval training should progressively move to shorter distances to replicate the time and intensity of points and matches you will play.

The second type of interval running programme aimed at improving your lactate tolerance involves longer periods of running interspersed with shorter recovery periods. This will improve your ability to withstand high levels of lactate without causing a reduction in work intensity.

Aerobic Training

This type of training is aimed at developing the efficiency of the heart and lungs in order to increase the amount of oxygen that can be transported to the muscles, as well as improve the ability of the muscles to take up and use oxygen.

For table tennis players this type of training is most suitable for use during the early part of pre-season training or as part of a rehabilitation programme following an injury. It involves mainly moderate intensity continuous running, although a combination of continuous and interval running can also be used known as 'Fartlek' running. It is necessary to raise the heart rate to about 70–80 per cent of your maximum heart rate in order to improve your aerobic fitness level. This is known as your ideal training zone.

Your maximum heart rate could be obtained by taking your pulse rate immediately after completing the 20-metre multi-stage fitness test, or your 'ideal training zone' can be calculated using the method shown in the information box on page 79.

In order to measure your heart rate you need to take your pulse rate; the two easiest places to obtain a pulse rate are in the

> **TOP TIP**
>
> An example of 'Fartlek' running would be to jog for 2 minutes, walk for 1 minute, jog for 2 minutes, sprint for 20 seconds, walk for 40 seconds. This sequence is then repeated four times, which gives a total of 24 minutes.

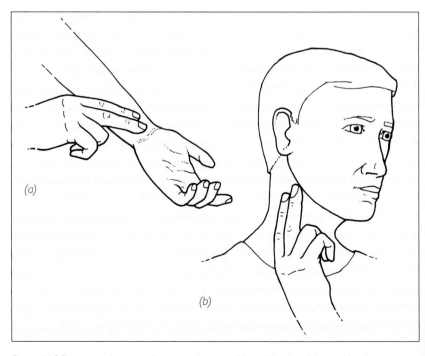

(a)

(b)

Figure 118 Two easy places to obtain a pulse rate: (a) radial pulse; (b) carotid pulse.

INFORMATION BOX

HOW TO CALCULATE YOUR IDEAL TRAINING ZONE

1. Maximum heart rate (MHR) = 220 − age
2. The ideal heart rate = 220 − age × percentage of MHR

Example: training zone for an active 20-year-old would be between 140 and 160

$220 - 20 = 200 \times 70$ per cent = 140
$220 - 20 = 200 \times 80$ per cent = 160

3. If however the 20-year-old was unfit, an extra 20 beats are deducted to obtain a more suitable training zone:

$220 - 20 - 20 = 180 \times 70$ per cent = 126
$220 - 20 - 20 = 180 \times 80$ per cent = 144

An ideal training zone between 126 and 144

4. Now calculate your own ideal training zone using the above formula.

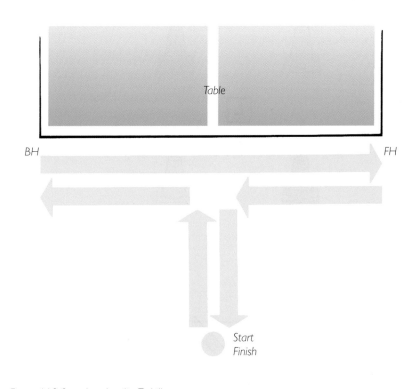

Figure 119 Speed and agility T drill.

wrist (radial pulse) and the neck (carotid pulse) (see Figure 118).

Speed and Agility Training

Speed and agility sessions involve very high intensity drills aimed at improving speed 'off the mark' and the ability to change direction rapidly. These sessions should be completed when feeling fresh to get the most out of them. The aim of this type of training is to increase neuromuscular co-ordination and efficiency of movement and in order to do this the drills are most beneficial if they are sport specific. There are a number of exercises that are used; included here are two slightly different examples used by the national squads.

The first one involves movements that are used in table tennis, plus the simulation of playing strokes as part of the drill. This exercise is often referred to as the T drill (see Figure 119). The direction taken by the participant in this drill is shown by the arrows; when the player is in front of the table they simulate a stroke at the BH and FH positions as indicated.

The second type of drill involves specific directional movements in response to a verbal or visual stimulus. The example used is referred to as 'big square, little square' (see Figure 120 overleaf). This drill requires two participants, one in the small square and the other in the big one. The participant in the small square (the leader) provides the stimulus for the other one to respond to. This stimulus can be verbal: the leader calls out a colour and the other participant moves and touches the appropriate coloured cone with their playing hand. The stimulus can also be visual: the leader holds up different coloured cards randomly and the other participant reacts to the stimulus by moving to the corresponding coloured cone and touching it with their playing hand. Alternatively the leader provides visual stimulus by simply moving to a particular cone in their small square and the other participant shadows this movement in the big square.

Maintaining and Increasing Flexibility

Flexibility can be maintained by regular exercises in which the joints are taken through a full stretch. Flexibility can only be increased, however, by overstretching in the same way that a muscle needs to be overloaded to increase strength.

Stretch exercises practised after a warm up will enhance performance and in a cool down will reduce muscle soreness and stiffness. To increase flexibility the stretching exercises need to be used as a complete programme. Static stretching is safer and more effective than ballistic stretching, as the tissues have time to relax in the former. In static stretching the muscle is moved slowly to the end of the range and held there. During the holding period, the muscle adapts to the stretch allowing an increase in muscle length. Static stretching may be classified as 'active' or 'passive'.

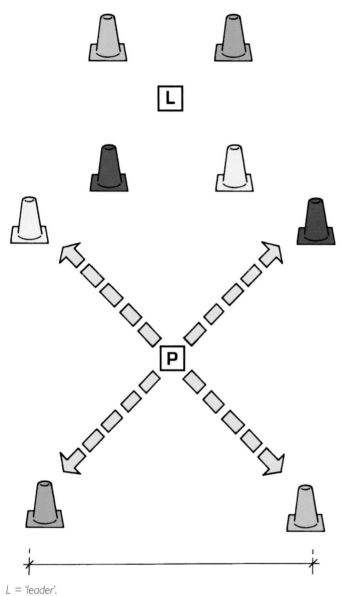

L = 'leader'.
P = 'performer'.

Figure 120 Speed and agility drill in response to a stimulus (big square, little square).

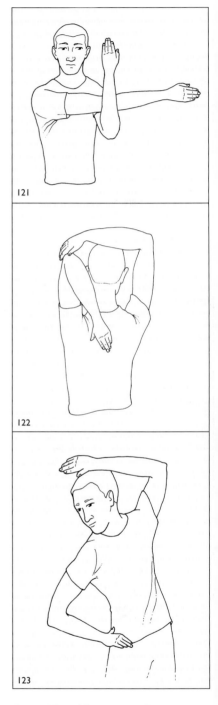

Active stretching refers to stretching without external aid, that is, by the participant themselves, but can be 'assisted' once the stretch has reached its limit by a partner applying pressure to gain a further stretch.

'Passive' stretching refers to a stretch by an external force, such as traction or by a partner, while the participant remains inactive.

Care should always be used and the stretch should be controlled and smooth.

Figures 121–130 Examples of static stretching exercises. Length of each hold and number of repetitions are for when you first start. These will need to be changed as you improve.

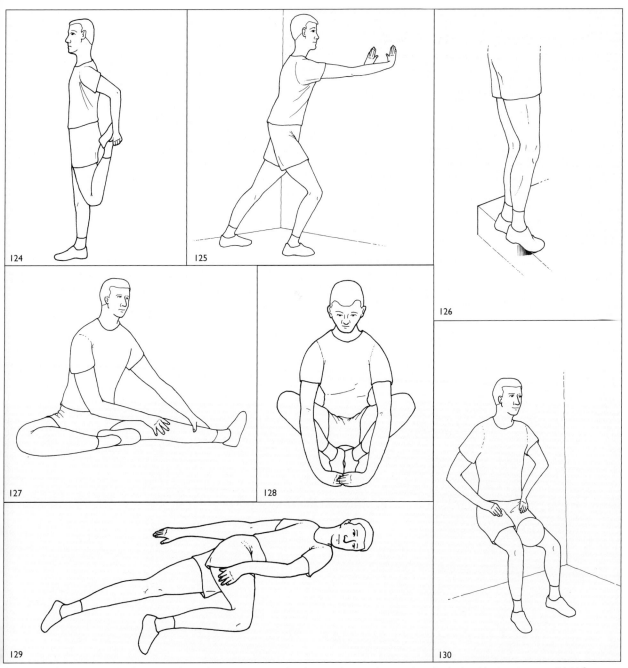

Figure 121 Shoulder stretch. Cross the elbow of one arm across the chest and press the arm into the body with the other arm. Hold for 10 seconds. Repeat twice on each arm. Figure 122 Shoulder, back and upper arm. Pull the elbow of one arm behind your head and press downward. Hold for 10 seconds. Repeat twice for each arm. Figure 123 Side stretch. With feet shoulder-width apart, extend one arm up and over the head whilst bending sideways. Hold for 10 seconds. Repeat five times for each arm. Figure 124 Quad stretch. Stand on one leg and bend the other up behind and gently pull the leg back until you feel the stretch in the quads. Hold for 20 seconds. Repeat twice for each leg. Figure 125 Calf stretch. Stand as shown with one leg forward and while keeping the heel of the rear foot on the ground, push against the wall. Hold for 20 seconds. Repeat twice for each leg. Figure 126 Calf and Achilles stretch. Take up the position shown and gently force the heels downwards. Hold for 5–10 seconds. Repeat five times. Figure 127 Seated hamstring stretch. One leg is extended and the other is pulled towards the groin. Slowly lean forwards but do not arch your back. Hold for 20 seconds. Repeat twice on each side. Figure 128 Groin stretch. Sit on the floor with the soles of the feet together and hold them with your hands. Keep your head up and bend from the hips until you feel the groin stretch. Hold for 10 seconds. Repeat twice. Figure 129 Lower back and side. Lie down on your back and bend your left leg to 90 degrees over the other leg. Stretch out the left arm so that the shoulder remains on the ground. Hold the left leg with your right hand for 20 seconds. Repeat twice for each leg. Figure 130 Wall slide (hamstrings, buttocks and abdominals). With your legs shoulder-width apart and a Swiss ball placed between your back and the wall and a smaller ball between your knees, slowly slide down the wall until your knees are bent at 90 degrees. Hold for 10 seconds. Repeat 10 times.

Strength and Power Training

This type of training can be used to develop muscle strength, bulk, endurance or explosive power. The most important ones for table tennis are strength, endurance and power. Too much bulk will hamper flexibility and speed of movement, and should be restricted in its use for table tennis.

The exercises used require you to work against a load or resistance and there are different types of resistance training. The load, number of repetitions, number of sets, speed of contraction and the rest period can all be varied to produce the desired effects. Muscles can be made to work against:

- Own body weight (callisthenics), such as in press ups, squat thrusts
- Resistance provided by a partner, such as pushing against them
- Free weights, like barbells and dumbbells
- Machine weights, such as gym equipment on which the load can be varied
- Plyometric training, where a muscle contraction follows a rapid stretch, such as rapid hopping, jumping or leaping.

Weight training should always be done under the supervision of an experienced practitioner so that you are taught the correct technique and provided with a training programme with the appropriate load, repetitions, sets and rest period combinations to suit you.

The use of plyometric training also needs expert tuition, as there is a danger of damaging joints or producing microtears in muscle fibres as a result of this type of exercising. For this reason most national team squads have an expert in 'strength and conditioning' working closely with them or as one of the coaches. All recognized gyms also have expert advice available so make sure you obtain it before starting a strength and power training programme.

Crossover step enables the player to cover the distance quicker as he moves to a wide ball.

CHAPTER 15

ON-THE-TABLE TRAINING

Types of Training

There are five main types of training on the table: regular, regular with some free play, irregular, irregular with some free play and multi-ball training.

On-the-table exercises using these different types of training have been used throughout this guide, particularly in Chapters 8, 9 and 10 to develop your technical game and in Chapters 11 and 12 to develop your tactical game.

Regular exercises are ones when both players hit the ball to a known target area on the table using a specific stroke, speed or spin, in a regular pattern; they are particularly useful for developing placement and technique.

A regular exercise with an element of free play is where a player knows how and where a ball will be played for a set number of strokes; and then after this the ball can be placed anywhere (free play). This type is particularly useful for developing tactical play.

Irregular exercises help the player to read their opponent's play from their racket angle, body movement, table position, direction and speed of the stroke because the placement of the ball is not pre-determined. These exercises are particularly good for practising the multi-directional changes that are needed in match-play and improving anticipation.

An irregular–free exercise is one that is initially irregular but with some constraints imposed, such as a specific service to anywhere in the forehand court followed by the ball being played anywhere. This closely resembles match-play but is used to practise specific aspects of your game.

Multi-ball is a method used for training at all levels. A coach or feeder delivers many balls to the player for them to practise a particular element of the game.

The feeder may deliver the ball in a regular or irregular pattern from close to the net, behind the table or from different sides of the table in order to change the angle. This is better than using a robot because the feeder can vary the speed, placement and spin imparted on each ball delivered in order to practise any aspect of the game. At the advanced stage of development, multi-ball is particularly useful for improving reaction time, footwork and speed of stroke frequency, and at the beginner stage for technique development.

Using multi-ball is also a good way of practising the return of service because the length and spin imparted can be controlled better. Practising your service only requires a table and a bag of balls.

Tactical play needs to be practised in competitive situations and so match-play is important as part of any training programme and to your long-term development as a player.

There are three distinct phases to your development that have to be continually repeated as you learn to increase your speed, spin and power, otherwise you will lose your ability to play consistently or accurately.

When starting to play table tennis, consistency, control and stroke development are the most important elements,

Kelly Sibley and Darius Knight team up in the mixed doubles competition at the English National Championships.

but as you get better you will increase the amount of spin and speed you put on the ball and this will at first result in loss of accuracy, control and placement. So each time you learn to use more spin, power or speed you will need to practise the other elements of your all-round game (see Figure 131).

Training Sessions

During a training session and as you progress, the type of exercises you will use will progressively move from regular, fixed-pattern ones to more irregular and match-play exercises.

Training in the world's élite countries in Asia and Europe varies. European countries, in general, favour sessions of about 2 hours with exercises lasting between 5 and 10 minutes of high-intensity work based on match-play, with short breaks between.

The Asian countries generally train much longer, with exercises often lasting 15–30 minutes with many fixed-position routines to master specific techniques.

Multi-ball training in European countries is often less than 10 per cent, whereas in Asia it is used more and constitutes about 30 per cent of training time.

Another method of training made popular in Norway is called 'Body Clock training' whereby the coach explains all the exercises at the start of the session and the players change when they feel ready, rather than after a fixed time.

It is important to use your training time well and you should divide the time in the session to include exercises to practise: control and placement, footwork, service and receive, tactics and match-play.

In the Swedish model, players complete the complex tactical and match-play exercises before fatigue reduces their effectiveness, that is, near to the middle of a session. Other models are planned to reflect a 'real competition' situation where the most important matches will be played at the end of a long day. In this type of model, match-play and tactical work are done nearer the end of a session.

Although there are different approaches used to training sessions throughout the world, what they all have in common is a clear plan as to what will be included and what the aim of each session is in order to maximize the use of the time.

No matter which model you adopt all sessions need to start with a warm up and finish with any physical training followed by a cool down. It is equally important to balance the use of regular and irregular exercises, and include footwork and service and receive exercises. In the early stages you should aim to use mostly regular exercises but as you improve, you should increase your use of irregular exercises and match-play. A typical 2-hour session plan for an improving player is shown in Table 11.

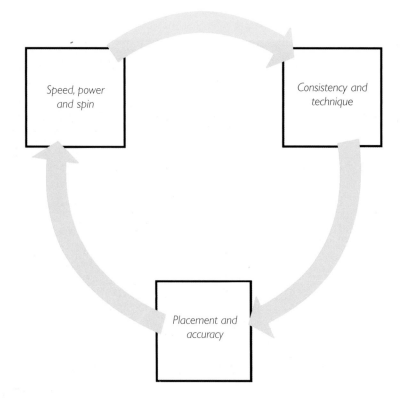

Figure 131 The cycle of stages needed for stroke and skill development.

TABLE 11: A SAMPLE 2-HOUR TABLE TENNIS SESSION FOR AN IMPROVING PLAYER	
Activity	Duration (minutes)
Warm up	15
Knock-up	5
Regular exercises (including control, placement and footwork)	40
Irregular exercises (anticipation, footwork and tactical placement)	20
Service and receive	15
Match-play	15
Cool down	10
	Total 120

Seasonal Planning

Planning your training schedule throughout the year is also important; this section provides some simple guidelines as to what you should include in both your on-the-table and fitness training programmes at different times of the year: pre-season, during the season and prior to a major tournament.

On-the-table Training: Seasonal Priorities

Pre-season
During your pre-season training sessions you should concentrate more on trying to improve your weaknesses and fitness.

- Use a lot of exercises with movement between forehand and backhand (combination exercises).
- Practise a lot of footwork.
- Practise mainly your weaknesses but do not exclude your strengths altogether.
- Experiment and practise your service and receive.

This period is the most important time of the season where a player can improve the most without the pressures of competition looming up. The results of working hard in this period will show dividends in the season.

During the Season

- Train more on your strengths.
- Practise more random play by using irregular exercises and exercises which will be free after regular placements.
- Footwork exercises should concentrate 50 per cent on playing FH from BH corner and 50 per cent combination work to practise sideways movements.
- Practise your ability to attack into the body (crossover point) as well as playing against a ball played into your body.
- Start with serve and return on 50 per cent of all exercises.

Leading up to an Important Tournament

- Train almost 100 per cent on your strengths.

Gavin Evans shows good sideways footwork to play a forehand topspin from the backhand side of the table.

- Exercises should concentrate on 'winning the point'.
- Start with serve and return in 60 per cent of all exercises.
- Include playing the FH from the BH corner in 70 per cent of all exercises.
- Use a lot of exercises into the body.
- Focus on exercises with serve and return, especially short and half long balls.
- Physical training should concentrate on speed work, maintenance and injury prevention.

Seasonal Fitness Training Priorities

During the early part of pre-season fitness training (the first 2–4 weeks) the key objective of most table tennis players should be to develop their aerobic base and capacity.

The volume and intensity of the aerobic capacity conditioning should be increased gradually. The introduction of more specific anaerobic and speed and agility training sessions should then be introduced and gradually increased as the volume of aerobic training is reduced.

As the competitive phase approaches, more physical conditioning should be done on the table using table tennis specific movement patterns.

However, for young athletes (under 16) the use of anaerobic training should be limited as their anaerobic energy systems are not equipped to deal with or adapt to too much of this type of work. Instead aerobic capacity training and short bouts of speed and agility training should be used, with more table tennis specific work to maintain the interest of the athlete.

During the competitive phase of the season, and particularly in the build up to important tournaments, the intensity of fitness training sessions should be for maintenance with a reduction in the length of each session to prevent fatigue.

Andrew Baggaley shows good use of the legs to generate the power to play a forehand topspin away from the table at the English National Championships in Sheffield.

CHAPTER 16

INJURY PREVENTION AND MANAGEMENT

Introduction

The risk of injury is always a possibility when playing any sport but provided you have a reasonable level of fitness, wear appropriate clothes and footwear, warm up before playing or training, follow a fitness programme showing gradual progression and have good technique, you shouldn't experience too many injuries.

If an injury does occur then it is important that you *stop* the activity and assess the situation. Attempting to diagnose or treat any injury without specialist medical training is to be avoided. However, knowing what action to take immediately before medical attention is available can reduce the extent of tissue damage.

If there is any bleeding then this needs to be stemmed by applying firm even pressure directly over the area using a sterile dressing.

If there is any suspicion that the injury is due to a fracture, then it is important not to move the affected area and to send for help.

If the injury is minor, such as just bruising, a minor cut or a bump then you should be safe to carry on.

For any soft tissue injury the RICER regime is useful for the prevention of further damage.

RICER refers to the following steps:

R – rest and immobilize the part injured
I – apply ice wrapped in a towel or bag but not directly to the skin as ice burns can occur
C – apply compression to the injured area by using a bandage
E – elevate the injured part (above the level of the heart if possible) to help drainage

R – refer the injury to a suitably qualified professional (such as a doctor) for diagnosis as soon as possible.

Types of Injury

Acute (traumatic) injuries happen suddenly because of some external force or internal stress and produce sudden pain, swelling, bruising or wounds.

Chronic injuries occur slowly and are usually due to overuse or repetition and progressively worsen over a period of time.

Muscle injuries are due to micro-tears (strains), partial tears or complete tears of the muscle fibres, and require different treatment regimes. A complete tear may require surgery.

> **TOP TIP**
>
> The fitter you are and the better your technique is, the less likely it is you will suffer from injury. Remember that if you have a long break from playing or training your fitness levels will need to be increased gradually as will the length of your training sessions if you are to avoid injury.

Tendon injuries are either tears of varying degrees, the worst being a rupture that may require surgery, or inflammation of the tendon (tendonitis) or the tendon in its sheath (tenosynovitis). Tendon tears are traumatic injuries and usually occur at the weakest point, which is where they join the muscle. Inflammation injuries are due to overuse or repetition but can occur by awkward

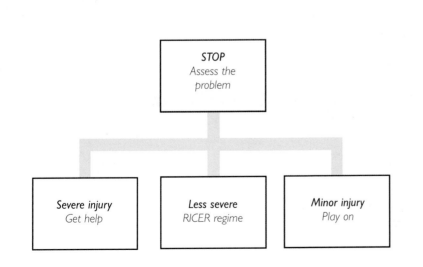

Figure 132 Injury management steps.

movements, such as miss-hitting a stroke (bad technique).

Ligaments attach bone to bone and are damaged when joints are forced into abnormal positions, for example twisting your ankle results in a sprained ligament. Ligaments can also suffer partial and complete tears and in extreme cases may require suturing.

Due to the nature of table tennis and the requirement to repeatedly change direction, sprains and strains are quite common, as are injuries due to repetitive movements and overuse in training and competitive play.

Some common injuries are listed in Table 12 with their possible causes and management.

TABLE 12: COMMON TYPES OF INJURY IN TABLE TENNIS

Injury	Possible cause	Management
Muscle strain, e.g. calf	Sudden overloading or over-stretching	Decrease activity RICER + slow static stretching Physiotherapy
Tendon tear, e.g. Achilles tendon	Traumatic injury	May require surgery RICER (less severe) Physiotherapy
Tennis elbow	Overuse, poor technique or change of grip	Decrease activity RICER Modify technique Physiotherapy
Ligament sprain, e.g. ankle	Abnormal or twisting movement	Decrease activity RICER + slow static stretching Physiotherapy
Skin soreness, e.g. feet	Poor footwear Poor-fitting socks or footwear Postural imbalance	Decrease any painful activity RICER as long as there are no blisters/abrasions Correct footwear Orthotic advice
Cramp, e.g. calf	Fatigue Loss of salts and body fluids	Straightening of the leg to stretch the muscles Keep the leg warm

Gavin Evans pushes off quickly to his right to reach a wide ball.

PART 5

HOW TO FIND OUT MORE

CHAPTER 17

ORGANIZATION OF TABLE TENNIS

The world national governing body for table tennis is the International Table Tennis Federation (ITTF), which is then divided into six continental areas. The UK National Governing Bodies of table tennis belong to the European Table Tennis Union (ETTU).

The UK home countries compete as separate nations in all table tennis competitions except the Olympics. The home countries each have their own national governing body responsible for the development of the sport from 'grass roots' to international level including the training of their own international squad players.

The umbrella association for table tennis in the UK is the British Table Tennis Federation (BTTF) which is responsible for the development of the best players selected from all the home countries in preparation for the Olympics. The main member countries are England, Northern Ireland, Wales and Scotland but players from the Channel Islands and Isle of Man are also eligible to be selected.

INTERNATIONAL TABLE TENNIS FEDERATION (ITTF)

The member associations belong to one of six continental associations. The numbers below each indicate the different associations registered in each.

Africa	Europe	North America	Oceania	Latin America	Asia
e.g. Nigeria Cameroon S. Africa	e.g. England Wales Scotland Ireland	e.g. USA Canada	e.g. Australia New Zealand	e.g. Brazil Argentina Chile	e.g. China Japan N. and S. Korea India
45	57	4	19	34	46

Figure 133 World organization of table tennis (ITTF).

ENGLISH TABLE TENNIS ASSOCIATION (ETTA)

Each of the nine regions has a committee, chair, coaching co-ordinator, development officer and coach.

South and southeast	Southwest	East	East Midlands	West Midlands	Yorkshire	North	Northwest	London
Berkshire Bucks Hampshire Isle of Wight Kent Oxfordshire Surrey Sussex	Avon Cornwall Devon Dorset Gloucestershire Somerset Wiltshire	Beds Cambs Herts Norfolk Suffolk Essex	Derbyshire Leicestershire Lincolnshire Northants Notts	Herefordshire Shropshire Staffordshire Warwickshire Worcestershire	S. Yorks N. Yorks	Cleveland Durham Northumberland	Cheshire Cumbria Lancs	Middlesex 33 boroughs

Figure 134 Organization of table tennis in England (ETTA).

CHAPTER 18

USEFUL ADDRESSES

The English Table Tennis Association
(ETTA)
3rd Floor, Queensbury House
Havelock Road, Hastings
East Sussex, TN34 1HF
Tel: 01424 722525
Fax: 01424 422103
Email: admin@englishtabletennis.org.uk
Website: www.englishtabletennis.org.uk

Table Tennis Scotland (TTS)
Caledonia House, South Gyle
Edinburgh, EH12 9DQ
Tel: 0131 3178077
Fax: 0131 317 8224
Website: www.tabletennisscotland.com

Irish Table Tennis Association
Sport HQ
13 Joyce Way, Park West, Dublin 12,
Ireland
Tel: 353 1 6251135
Fax: 353 1 6521136
Website: www.irishtabletennis.com

Irish Table Tennis Association, Ulster
(ITTA (Ulster))
House of Sport, Upper Malone Road
Belfast, BT9 5LA
Tel: 028 90383811
Email: jingyi@ttulster.co.uk
Website: www.irishtabletennis.com/ulster

Table Tennis Association of Wales
(TTAW)
E mail: admin@ttaw.co.uk
Website: www.ttaw.co.uk

Table Tennis Australia Incorporated
Office 2.02 Sports House, 150 Caxton
Street,
Milton QLD 4064
Australia
Tel: 61 7 3369 4999
E mail: ao@tabletennis.org.au
Website: www.tabletennis.org.au

Table Tennis Canada
2211 Riverside Drive, Suite 308
Ottowa ON K1H 7X5
Canada
Tel: 613 7336272
Email: ctta@ctta.ca
Website: www.ctta.ca

Table Tennis New Zealand
PO Box 867, Wellington,
New Zealand
Tel: 64 4 9162459
Email: ttnz@tabletennis.org.nz
Website: www.tabletennis.org.nz

South African Table Tennis Board
PO Box 14510, Clubview, Centurion 0014
Republic of South Africa
Email: sattb@yebo.co.za
Website: www.tabletennis.co.za

USA Table Tennis
1 Olympic Plaza, Colorada Springs,
CO 80909-5769,
USA
Tel: 719 866 4583
Email: ed@usatt.org
Website: www.usatt.org

Other Useful Websites and emails

International Table Tennis Federation
www.ittf.com
European Table Tennis Union
www.ettu.org
African Table Tennis Federation
www.africanttf.com
Asian Table Tennis Union
www.attu.org
Oceania Table Tennis Federation
www.ottf.org
Jersey Table Tennis Association
edleq@jerseymail.co.uk
Guernsey Table Tennis Association
GTTAsecretary@cwgsy.net
Isle of Man Table Tennis Association
iomtta@googlemail.com
English Schools Table Tennis Association
www.estta.org.uk

GLOSSARY

Anti-spin   A rubber type that counters spin and speed.

Backhand   The side of the bat with the first finger showing in a shake hands grip.

Backspin   Produced by brushing the ball downwards so that the ball rotates backwards.

Blade   The part of the racket made mainly of wood without the covering.

Block   A stroke used to control spin and speed using a closed bat angle.

Blocker   A style of play in which blocking is the main stroke used.

Chop   A backspin stroke played away from the table.

Chopper   A style of play in which the player uses a variation of backspin strokes.

Cool down   A short session following training or competition aimed at preventing soreness and injury.

Counter-spin   A stroke in which topspin is returned using topspin.

Cross-court   A ball which is hit diagonally from corner to corner.

Crossover   A style of footwork used to cover larger distances quickly.

Crossover point   The area near the right hip where it is difficult for a player to decide whether to use a forehand or backhand.

Deep   A ball that would not bounce twice on the opponent's side of the table if given the chance to do so.

Deuce   When the score is 10-all and service changes every point until one player is two points clear of his/her opponent and has won the game.

Double bounce   A ball that hits the same side of the table twice before being returned. The person on that side loses the point.

Doubles   A format in table tennis where two people play as a pair on each side of the table and must alternate at striking the ball.

Down the line   A ball hit parallel to the side lines.

Drive   A stroke played with a closed bat angle hitting the back of the ball in an upward direction.

Drop shot   A surprise stroke played very short when an opponent is positioned away from the table.

Expedite rule   After a time limit has expired during a game the receiver wins the point if he/she returns the ball successfully 13 times in a row.

Flick   A stroke played against a short service using a fast wrist action in an upward direction.

Footwork   How the player moves into position to play a stroke.

Forehand   The side of the bat with the thumb when using a shake hands grip.

Free hand   The hand not holding the bat and which is important in balance.

Game   Is usually the first player to reach 11 points unless deuce has been reached in which case it is not over until one player is two points clear of their opponent.

Hard rubber   A type of racket covering without a sponge layer.

International Table Tennis Federation   The world governing body for the sport, based in Lausanne, Switzerland.

Let   A stoppage of play as a result of the serve hitting the net and going over or as a result of interference from outside the court.

Lob   A high topspin return played well back from the table usually in response to a smash.

Long pimples   A rubber whose surface consists of fairly long pimples which produces unpredictable spin.

Loop   An attacking stroke used to produce a lot of topspin.

Looper   A style of play in which the main stroke used is the loop.

Match   Consists of the best of any odd number of games, usually best of 3, 5 or 7.

Penhold   A type of grip used mainly in Asia where the bat is held like a pen or chopsticks.

Playing surface   The top of the table, including the edges, which can be any dark, matt colour but the most commonly used colours are green and blue.

Point   Is won when an opponent fails to hit the ball over or round the net so that it lands on the top or edge, on your side of table.

Push   A stroke used for control, which is produced using an open bat angle.

Racket   The alternative and correct name for the bat.

Racket hand   The hand that is used to hold the racket (bat).

Rally   The hitting of the ball back and forth, starting with a serve and ending when the point is won.

Rating   A number assigned to a player after their first tournament. The higher the rating a player has the better the player should be.

Receive   The return of the service.

Reverse backhand topspin   A topspin stroke played by penhold players where the reverse side of the grip is used rather than the normal side to produce a topspin attacking stroke.

Rubber   The covering put onto the blade usually with a layer of sponge underneath it.

Server   The player who starts a rally.

Service   The beginning of a rally where one player strikes the ball onto his/her own side of the table first after the ball has been thrown upwards from the palm of the free hand.

Shake hands   A type of grip where the racket is held with the middle, ring and little finger wrapped around the handle and the first finger resting on the back of the racket.

Short A stroke or service that given the opportunity would bounce at least twice on the opponent's side of the table.

Sidespin A type of spin produced by brushing the ball from right to left or left to right producing a sideways rotation.

Sidestepping The most commonly used footwork in table tennis, particularly when close to the table.

Smash An attacking stroke used against a high bouncing ball and struck downwards at high speed.

Speed glue A type of glue that is applied between the sponge and blade which makes the ball faster and spinnier.

Spin The direction the ball rotates after contact with the bat.

Sponge The layer of bouncy material attached to the back of the rubber. The use of sponge ended the 'hard rubber' age in the 1950s and both made the game faster and allowed a greater use of spin.

Stroke The method by which the ball is struck by a player with the racket, including the service.

Topspin A type of spin produced by brushing the ball upwards using a closed bat angle that results in the ball rotating away from the player.

Umpire The official who keeps score and enforces the rules during a match.

Volley To hit the ball before it bounces on your side of the table, which will result in you losing the point.

Warm up The session prior to training or competition, which is aimed at preparing you both physically and mentally.

The concentration required during the service action is clear to see.

The European Top 10 tournament for cadet and junior boys and girls held in Sheffield.

INDEX